# 5-Ingredient Cooking for Two

# 60 Days of Healthy Breakfast Recipes

By

APRIL KELSEY

## Copyright © 2024

All rights reserved. No part of this book may be reproduced, stored in a retrieval system, or transmitted in any form or by any means, electronic, mechanical, photocopying, recording, scanning, or otherwise, without the publisher's prior written permission.

## Disclaimer

The material in this book is provided for educational and informational purposes only. No responsibility can be taken for any results or outcomes from using this material.

While every attempt has been made to provide accurate and effective information, the author does not assume any responsibility for its accuracy or use/misuse.

**ALL RIGHTS RESERVED.** No part of this publication may be reproduced or transmitted in any form, electronic or mechanical, including photocopying, recording, or by any informational storage or retrieval system without express written, dated, and signed permission from the author.

Copyright © 2024 April Kelsey
All rights reserved.
**ISBN:** 9798321074961

# CONTENTS

| | |
|---|---|
| Introduction | 8 |
| Why Only Cook For Two? | 9 |
| Why Is the Concept of Only 5-Ingredient Popular? | 10 |
| Tips for Grocery Shopping and Meal Planning For Two | 12 |
| Toasted Avocado Egg Duo | 14 |
| Greek Yogurt Berry Medley | 16 |
| Grab-and-Go Egg Delights | 19 |
| Fluffy Oatmeal Banana Pancakes | 22 |
| Garden Veggie Delight Omelette | 25 |
| Smoky Salmon Breakfast Bagel | 28 |
| Leafy Green Egg Cups | 30 |
| Sizzling Sausage Crescent Casserole | 32 |
| Avocado Breakfast Delight | 35 |
| Classic Ham and Swiss Fold | 38 |
| Sunrise Fruit Parfait | 41 |
| Ham and Egg Breakfast Roll | 44 |
| Italian Egg Meringue | 47 |
| Cinnamon Apple Oats in a Jar | 50 |
| Breakfast Caprese Egg Sandwich | 52 |
| Morning Sweet Potato Delight | 54 |
| Fruity Waffle Parfaits | 56 |
| Banana Flip Pancakes | 58 |
| Waffle Breakfast Sandwich | 60 |
| Salsa-Infused Scramble | 62 |

| | |
|---|---|
| Southern Egg Sandwich | 64 |
| Bagel Bonanza Banana | 66 |
| Creamy Herb Omelette | 68 |
| Express Spinach Omelette | 71 |
| Egg Provolone Panini | 74 |
| Smoky Salmon Breakfast Scramble | 77 |
| Oatmeal Banana Hotcakes | 79 |
| Rhubarb Yogurt Parfait | 82 |
| Peanut Butter Banana Breakfast Delight | 85 |
| Egg and Toast Soldiers | 88 |
| Breakfast Bread Cup | 91 |
| Sausage Cheese Breakfast Wrap | 93 |
| Ricotta Bean Bruschetta Toast | 96 |
| Fruity Nut Oatmeal Mix | 98 |
| Crunchy Cornflake Bacon | 101 |
| Orange French Toast Delight | 104 |
| Mushroom Spinach Egg Pie | 106 |
| Blueberry Bliss Yogurt Bowl | 109 |
| Berry Burst Chia Pudding | 111 |
| Banana Nut Oatmeal Delight | 113 |
| Coconut Milk Nutty Oats | 115 |
| Bacon Cheddar Breakfast Cups | 117 |
| Berrylicious Muesli Trio | 120 |
| Raspberries and Oats Delight | 122 |
| Mushroom Spinach Egg Scramble | 124 |
| Egg Chorizo Breakfast Wraps | 126 |

| | |
|---|---:|
| Quick Egg Cheese Delight | 128 |
| Ham and Cheese Breakfast Bun | 130 |
| Mascarpone Berry Toast Treat | 132 |
| Almond Butter Grape Delight | 134 |
| Sunny-Side Up Open-Face Breakfast | 137 |
| Lentil Goat Cheese Morning Melt | 139 |
| Simple Cereal Snack Bars | 141 |
| Sweet Bacon Grits Puff | 144 |
| Blueberry Muffin French Delight | 146 |
| Southwest Breakfast Burrito Bowl | 148 |
| Feta Egg Breakfast Burritos | 150 |
| Spicy Salsa Chorizo Omelette | 153 |
| Breakfast Bacon Pizza | 155 |
| Creamy Polenta Breakfast Delight | 158 |
| Minty Melon Smoothie | 161 |
| Kale Chickpea Morning Mix | 163 |
| Sausage Pancake Breakfast Bake | 166 |
| Ricotta-Berry Crepes | 169 |

# Introduction

In today's world, after a hectic day in the office, the last thing any couple wants is to spend hours in the kitchen preparing dinner. They prefer quick meals that allow them to relax and savor valuable time with loved ones.

Couples nowadays want simple recipes with fewer ingredients but still packed with flavor. They're looking for easy, tasty, healthy meals that simplify their lives. This trend towards more straightforward cooking with fewer ingredients has become quite popular.

We have the ideal solution for couples who love tasty meals but hate the hassle of cooking and cleaning up. With 5-Ingredient Cooking, you can whip up flavorful dishes that fit your busy schedule, whether a hectic weeknight or a weekend. These recipes are simple and easy, perfect for busy couples. They're tasty and suit active lifestyles.

# Why Only Cook For Two?

Cooking for two has become famous for several reasons. Many households consist of smaller families or couples living alone. So, make recipes tailored for two that are more practical and efficient.

Cooking for two reduces food waste by making just enough for a meal. It also creates intimate dining moments for couples to bond.

It's also cost-effective, as recipes can be scaled down to fit the needs of a smaller household, reducing grocery expenses.

*Portion control helps avoid overeating and reduces the desire to eat inappropriate food. By regulating calorie intake, it aids in weight management and improves general well-being.* By controlling portions, you can maintain a balanced diet and feel satisfied, leading to a healthier lifestyle.

Cooking for two is a great way to make meals that suit smaller households. It's practical, efficient, and simple to plan and cook. It meets the needs and preferences of many modern homes.

# Why Is the Concept of Only 5-Ingredient Popular?

The concept of 5-Ingredient Cooking has gained popularity for several reasons.

It offers simplicity and efficiency in the kitchen. With five ingredients, recipes become easier to follow. It means less shopping, chopping, and cooking time. Busy individuals and families like quick, hassle-free meal solutions. They find this simplicity appealing.

5-Ingredient Cooking cuts food waste. With fewer ingredients, you'll use pantry staples, reducing the chances of wasted ingredients.

Furthermore, 5-ingredient recipes often focus on natural flavors and wholesome ingredients. With fewer components in a dish, each ingredient shines. Its make meals more delicious and satisfying.

Moreover, the 5-Ingredient Concept is versatile and adaptable. It allows for kitchen creativity. Cooks can experiment with ingredient combos to create various dishes. This flexibility makes 5-Ingredient Cooking suitable for all cuisines and dietary preferences.

The rise of 5-ingredient Cooking is due to its simplicity. It's efficient, emphasizes quality ingredients, and offers versatility. This makes it attractive for cooks at any skill level.

# Tips for Grocery Shopping and Meal Planning For Two

When grocery shopping and meal planning for two. Proper planning is important. Here are tips for easy meal planning for the week:

- **Plan Your Meals:** Spend some time organizing your meals every week. Think about your nutrition, timetable, and any ingredients you already have. Planning ahead prevents rushed choices and guarantees meal prep success.
- **Create a Shopping List**: By your diet. Make a shopping list with all the ingredients you'll need for the upcoming week. Organize your list by category, such as produce, dairy, and pantry staples. This will make the grocery store easier to navigate. Stick to your list to avoid impulse purchases and unnecessary items.
- **Shop smart:** When grocery shopping, choose fresh, seasonal produce. Opt for processed foods when you can. Take advantage of sales and discounts. Use them to save money on basics like grains, beans, and canned goods. Consider purchasing items in bulk or larger

quantities to save money in the long run.
- **Consider portion sizes.** Adjust recipes to avoid food waste when planning meals. Look for recipes that can easily be scaled down to two servings or enjoyed as leftovers for future meals.
- **Embrace Versatile Ingredients:** Choose ones you can use in many meals all week. This gives you most flexibility. For example, a rotisserie chicken can be used in salads, sandwiches, or pasta dishes. A bag of frozen vegetables can be added to soups, stir-fries, or grain bowls.
- **Stay Organized:** Keep your pantry, fridge, and freezer well-organized. This makes meal prep and planning easier. Label your leftovers with dates. So you can use them before they spoil. Invest in storage containers to keep ingredients fresh.

# Toasted Avocado Egg Duo

- **Prep Time**: 10 minutes
- **Cook Time**: 5 minutes
- **Total Time**: 15 minutes
- **Servings**: 2
- **Calories**: 320

## Ingredients:

- 2 ripe avocados
- 4 slices of whole-grain bread
- 2 eggs
- Salt and pepper to taste
- Optional: red pepper flakes or hot sauce for garnish.

## Instructions:

- First, half-ripe avocados and remove the pits. Transfer the flesh to a bowl and mash it with a fork until smooth. Add some pepper and salt for seasoning.
- Toast whole-grain bread until golden.
- Next, Preheat a non-stick skillet over medium heat while the bread toasts.
- Once the skillet is hot, add the eggs and cook until they are the desired doneness (fried or scrambled).
- Now, distribute the mashed avocado in an even layer on each toasted piece of bread.

- Place a cooked egg on top of each avocado toast.
- Add salt, pepper, red pepper flakes, and hot sauce for seasoning if preferred.
- Serve the avocado toast with an egg immediately.

## Variations:

- **Spicy Twist:** add diced jalapeños to the mashed avocado.
- **Herbed Delight:** To add flavor to mashed avocado, chop fresh herbs such as cilantro, parsley, or chives and mix them in.
- **Cheese Lover's Dream:** Sprinkle shredded cheese over the mashed avocado before adding the cooked egg for an extra cheesy indulgence.
- **Tomato Basil Upgrade:** Top each avocado toast with sliced tomatoes and fresh basil leaves for a pop of freshness.
- **Seasoning Everything:** Add a dash of everything seasoning to the mashed avocado to give it a delicious twist.

# Greek Yogurt Berry Medley

- **Prep Time**: 10 minutes
- **Servings**: 2
- **Calories**: Approximately 200

## Ingredients:

- 1 cup Greek yogurt
- 1 cup mixed berries (such as strawberries, blueberries, and raspberries)
- 1/4 cup granola
- 1 tablespoon honey (optional)
- Fresh mint leaves for garnish (optional)

## Instructions:

- First, using a paper towel, wipe the berries clean and pat them dry.
- If the strawberries you use are particularly large, cut them into smaller pieces.
- To start making the parfait, choose your serving glasses or bowls.
- Start by adding a scoop of Greek yogurt to each glass or bowl. Next, add the mixed berries to the yogurt. Strawberries add color and tartness that complements creamy yogurt.

- Next, add a layer of granola. The granola adds texture and crunch to the parfait and serves as a delicious and healthy source of fiber.
- Continue layering the yogurt, berries, and granola until the container is complete, with a final layer of granola on top.
- For extra sweetness, drizzle honey over the granola.
- Garnish the parfaits with fresh mint leaves for a pop of color and freshness.
- Serve immediately and enjoy it as a nutritious breakfast, snack, or dessert.

## Variations:

- **Nutty Crunch:** Replace granola with chopped nuts like almonds, walnuts, or pecans for a crunch and protein boost.
- **Chocolate Indulgence:** Sprinkle dark chocolate chips or cocoa nibs between the layers for a decadent treat.
- **Tropical Paradise:** For a cool twist, try using tropical fruits like mango, pineapple, and kiwi instead of mixed berries.
- **Coconut Bliss:** Layer shredded coconut with yogurt

and berries for a tropical flavor profile.
- **Protein Powerhouse:** Stir protein powder into the Greek yogurt before layering to increase the protein content and make it more filling.

# Grab-and-Go Egg Delights

- **Prep Time:** 10 minutes
- **Cook Time:** 20 minutes
- **Total Time**: 30 minutes
- **Servings:** 2
- **Calories**: approximately 120

## Ingredients:

- 3 large eggs
- 2 tablespoons milk (or a dairy-free alternative)
- Salt and pepper to taste
- 1/4 cup chopped vegetables (such as bell peppers, spinach, onions, or tomatoes)
- 1/4 cup shredded cheese (such as cheddar, mozzarella, or feta)

## Instructions:

- Preheat the oven to 350°F (175°C). Use silicone muffin cups or grease a muffin tin.
- In a mixing bowl, crack the eggs. Next, add milk and season with pepper and salt. Mix the ingredients well.
- Next, add some chopped vegetables and shredded cheese to the egg mixture. Mix the vegetables and cheese into the egg mixture until evenly distributed.
- Now, fill each cup about 3/4 of the way up, as the egg

bites will rise as they bake.

- Once you have filled all the muffin cups, place the tin inside the oven for 15–20 minutes or cook until set and golden brown.
- Remove egg bites from the muffin tin after a few minutes. Use a butter knife or small spatula to remove egg bites from the pan.
- Serve warm, and enjoy a delicious breakfast or snack.

## Variations:

- **Meat Lover's Delight:** Add cooked bacon, ham, sausage, or turkey sausage crumbles to the egg mixture for a protein-packed option.
- **Mediterranean Twist:** Mix chopped olives, sun-dried tomatoes, and feta cheese into the egg mixture for a Mediterranean flavor profile.
- **Tex-Mex Flair:** Add diced green chilies, black beans, corn kernels, and shredded pepper jack cheese for a spicy twist.
- **Herbaceous Delight:** For freshness and flavor, fold in chopped fresh herbs such as parsley, chives, basil, or dill.

- **Veggie Medley:** Experiment with various vegetables, such as mushrooms, zucchini, broccoli, or asparagus, to create your veggie-packed combination.

# Fluffy Oatmeal Banana Pancakes

- **Prep Time:** 10 minutes
- **Cook Time:** 10 minutes
- **Total Time:** 20 minutes
- **Servings:** 2
- **Calories**: Approximately 200

## Ingredients:

- 1 ripe banana
- 1/2 cup rolled oats
- 1/4 cup milk (dairy or plant-based)
- 1 egg
- 1/2 teaspoon baking powder

## Instructions:

- To begin, mash a ripe banana in a mixing bowl until it reaches a smooth consistency. Add some rolled oats to this mixture and thoroughly stir to combine.
- Whisk the egg and milk together until smooth and combined. Once ready, pour the mixture into the bowl with the mashed banana and oats. Add baking powder to this mixture and stir until you get a thick batter well combined.
- Heat a nonstick skillet or griddle over medium heat. A small amount of butter or oil. For each pancake, add 1/4

cup of batter to the skillet. Cook until bubbles form on one side for 2–3 minutes. Next, use a spatula to flip the pancakes and cook for 1-2 minutes until they are golden brown and fully cooked. Repeat with the remaining batter.
- Remove the pancakes from the pan and place them on the platter.
- Add your favorite toppings, such as sliced bananas, berries, maple syrup, yogurt, or nut butter, to make your pancakes even more delicious.

## Variations:

- **Chocolate Chip Delight:** Stir chocolate chips into the batter for a more decadent treat.
- **Nutty Crunch:** Add chopped almonds, walnuts, or pecans for flavor and texture.
- **Berry Blast:** Fold in fresh or frozen berries, such as blueberries, raspberries, or strawberries, into the batter before cooking.
- **Coconut Paradise:** Sprinkle shredded coconut on the pancakes while they cook for a tropical twist.
- **Pumpkin Spice Flair:** Replace the banana with

pumpkin puree and add pumpkin pie spice for a seasonal variation.

# Garden Veggie Delight Omelette

- **Prep Time:** 5 minutes
- **Cook Time:** 10 minutes
- **Total Time:** 15 minutes
- **Calories**: approximately 220

## Ingredients:

- 3 large eggs
- 1/4 cup diced bell peppers (any color)
- 1/4 cup diced onions
- 1/4 cup diced tomatoes
- 1/4 cup shredded cheese (cheddar, mozzarella, or your choice)

## Instructions:

- First, dice the bell peppers, onions, and tomatoes into small pieces.
- Now, whisk the eggs in a bowl until they are well beaten, and season them with salt and pepper to taste.
- Next, heat the butter or oil in a pan over medium heat. Once heated, add chopped onions and bell peppers to the skillet and simmer until the vegetables are soft, 2 to 3 minutes.
- Next, add chopped tomatoes and simmer for 1–2 minutes. When tender, remove the vegetables from the

skillet and set aside.
- Pour beaten eggs into the same skillet with more butter or oil if needed. Swirl the eggs in the skillet to spread them evenly. Allow the eggs to cook for one to two minutes, or until the edges begin to set, without stirring.
- Now, sprinkle the sautéed vegetables evenly over one-half of the omelet. Sprinkle shredded cheese over the vegetables. Fold the omelet gently over the cheese and veggies with a spatula.
- Continue cooking the folded omelet for 1–2 minutes until the cheese melts and it's done.
- Slide the omelet onto a plate and serve it hot to enjoy a delicious and healthy veggie omelet with cheese.

## Variations:

- **Spinach and Feta Twist:** Substitute bell peppers, onions, and tomatoes with sautéed spinach and crumbled feta cheese for a Mediterranean-inspired omelet.
- **Mushroom Madness:** Add sliced mushrooms to the sautéed vegetables for an earthy flavor and extra nutrients.

- **Mexican Fiesta:** Mix in some diced jalapeños, black beans, and corn kernels for a spicy and hearty omelet. Top with salsa and avocado for an extra kick.
- **Italian Delight:** Use diced sun-dried tomatoes, olives, and fresh basil for an Italian-inspired omelet. Sprinkle with Parmesan cheese before folding.
- **Asian Fusion:** Stir-fry thinly sliced bell peppers, onions, and mushrooms with soy sauce and sesame oil. Fill the omelet with the stir-fried vegetables and sprinkle with sesame seeds for an Asian twist.

(Note: Nutritional values are approximate and may vary depending on specific ingredients and portion sizes.)

# Smoky Salmon Breakfast Bagel

- **Prep Time:** 5 minutes
- **Cook Time:** N/A
- **Total Time:** 5 minutes
- **Servings:** 2
- **Calories**: Approximately 280

## Ingredients:
- 2 bagels
- 2 ounces of smoked salmon
- 2 tablespoons of cream cheese
- 1 tablespoon capers
- 1 tablespoon red onion, thinly sliced

## Instructions:

- First, slice the bagels in half using a sharp knife. Slice them evenly to toast evenly.
- After cutting the bagels into thin slices, toast them in an oven or toaster until golden.
- Next, spread one tablespoon of cream cheese on each half of the toasted bagels.
- Add equal amounts of smoked salmon and cream cheese to each bagel half. Distribute it evenly.
- Now add the capers. Sprinkle them on each bagel half's smoked salmon. (If capers are unavailable, use chopped

pickles or olives.)
- Lastly, arrange the red onion slices over the capers.
- Your smoked salmon bagel with cream cheese is now ready to enjoy!

## Variations:

- **Avocado Addition:** Add slices of avocado for extra creaminess and flavor.
- **Everything Bagel Seasoning:** For a taste and texture boost, sprinkle everything bagel seasoning over the cream cheese.
- **Herb Infusion:** Mix chopped fresh herbs like dill, chives, or parsley into the cream cheese for a herby twist.
- **Spicy Kick:** Mix some red pepper flakes or a small hot sauce for a spicy kick.
- **Pickled Red Onion:** Use pickled red onion instead of raw onion for a tangy twist.

(Note: Nutritional values are approximate and may vary depending on specific ingredients and portion sizes.)

# Leafy Green Egg Cups

- **Prep Time:** 10 minutes
- **Cook Time:** 20 minutes
- **Total Time:** 30 minutes
- **Servings:** 2
- **Calories**: approximately 180

## Ingredients:

- 4 large eggs
- 1 cup fresh spinach, chopped
- 1/4 cup crumbled feta cheese
- 1/4 teaspoon garlic powder
- Salt and pepper to taste

## Instructions:

- First, preheat your oven to 350°F (175°C). Once the stove preheats, grease a muffin tin or line it with paper liners to ensure the egg muffins won't stick to the tin.
- Break an egg into a bowl and whisk it. Next, add the chopped spinach, crumbled feta cheese, garlic powder, salt, and pepper, and whisk it properly again.
- Next, pour the egg mixture into each muffin cup to fill it 3/4 full.
- Bake the muffin tin for 20–25 minutes to set and golden the egg muffins.

- Insert a toothpick into the middle of one muffin and check to see if it comes out clean.
- Remove the egg muffins from the oven and transfer them to a wire rack to cool completely.
- Serve it warm or at room temperature.

## Variations:

- **Mediterranean Twist:** To add a taste of the Mediterranean, chop some sun-dried tomatoes and Kalamata olives.
- **Mexican Flair:** Mix in some diced jalapeños and top with a sprinkle of shredded cheddar cheese for a spicy kick.
- **Italian Influence:** Incorporate chopped fresh basil and cherry tomatoes for an Italian-inspired version.
- **Protein Boost:** Add cooked and crumbled breakfast sausage or bacon bits for extra protein.
- **Veggie Delight:** For a veggie-packed option, include vegetables like diced bell peppers, mushrooms, or onions.

(Note: Nutritional values may vary depending on the specific ingredients used.)

# Sizzling Sausage Crescent Casserole

- **Prep Time:** 15 minutes
- **Cook Time:** 25 minutes
- **Total Time:** 40 minutes
- **Servings:** 2
- **Calories**: Approximately 500

## Ingredients:

- 4 breakfast sausage links
- 1 tube of refrigerated crescent roll dough
- 1 cup shredded cheddar cheese
- 4 large eggs
- 1/4 cup of milk
- Salt and pepper to taste
- Optional: chopped green onions or parsley for garnish.

## Instructions:

- Preheat the oven to 375°F (190°C).

- Grease or line a 13x9 baking dish with parchment paper to prepare it.

- Cook the breakfast sausage links in a skillet over medium heat until browned and fully cooked, and slice into bite-sized pieces after cooling slightly.

- Take the crescent roll dough and unroll it into the bottom of the baking dish, sealing any seams by pressing them together

- Sprinkle cooked sausage pieces and shredded cheddar cheese over the crescent roll dough.
- Next, mix eggs and milk in a bowl and stir the mixture with a whisk until it's smooth. Add a pinch of salt and pepper and stir.
- Spread the egg mixture uniformly over the sausage and cheese.
- Place the baking dish in the oven and bake it for approximately 20 to 25 minutes until the eggs are cooked and the crust, made of crescent rolls, turns golden brown.
- Remove from the oven and cool for a few minutes before slicing.
- If desired, garnish with finely chopped parsley or green onions.
- Serve warm, and enjoy your delicious sausage and crescent roll breakfast casserole!

## Variations:

- **Vegetarian Option:** Omit the sausage and add sautéed vegetables like bell peppers, onions, and mushrooms to make a vegetarian version.

- **Spicy Kick:** Add diced jalapeños or a sprinkle of red pepper flakes to the egg mixture for a spicy twist.
- **Cheesy Upgrade:** Mix in additional cheeses like pepper jack or Swiss for extra cheesy goodness.
- **Herb Infusion:** To flavor the egg mixture, add chopped fresh herbs like parsley, chives, or thyme.
- **Southwestern Flavor:** Add cooked black beans, diced tomatoes, and a dash of taco seasoning for a Tex-Mex-inspired casserole.

(Note: Nutritional values may vary depending on the ingredients used.)

# Avocado Breakfast Delight

- **Prep Time:** 5 minutes
- **Cook Time:** 5 minutes
- **Total Time:** 10 minutes
- **Servings:** 2
- **Calories**: Approximately 200

## Ingredients:

- 2 slices of your favorite bread (such as whole grain or sourdough)
- 1 ripe avocado
- 1 tablespoon everything bagel seasoning
- 1 teaspoon of lemon juice
- Salt and pepper to taste
- Optional toppings: sliced tomatoes, red pepper flakes, microgreens

## Instructions:

- Toast the bread slices for a few minutes until they turn golden brown and crisp.
- Next, cut the avocado in half and remove the pit. Then, use a spoon to scoop the avocado flesh into a bowl.
- Next, mash the avocado with a fork until its texture gets smooth and creamy.
- Stir in the bagel seasoning, lemon juice, salt, and pepper into the mashed avocado until well combined.

- Spread the seasoned avocado mixture evenly onto the toasted bread slices.
- To add flavor and texture, arrange sliced tomatoes, red pepper flakes, or microgreens on top of the avocado toast.
- Add sliced tomatoes, red pepper flakes, or microgreens to your avocado toast for a delicious twist.
- Serve when ready, and enjoy!

## Variations:

- **Fantastic Addition:** Place a fried or poached egg on top of each avocado toast for extra protein and richness.
- **She smoked Salmon Sensation:** Layer slices of smoked salmon on top of the avocado toast for a gourmet twist.
- **Cheese Lover's Dream:** Sprinkle shredded cheese (cheddar or feta) over the avocado mixture before toasting for a cheesy delight.
- **Mediterranean Influence:** For a Mediterranean-inspired flavor, add sliced olives, sun-dried tomatoes, and balsamic glaze.
- **Spicy Kick:** Mix some sriracha or hot sauce into the

mashed avocado for a spicy kick.

(Note: Nutritional values may vary depending on the ingredients used.)

# Classic Ham and Swiss Fold

- **Prep Time:** 5 minutes
- **Cook Time:** 5 minutes
- **Total Time:** 10 minutes
- **Servings:** 2
- **Calories**: Approximately 250

## Ingredients:

- 4 large eggs
- 1/4 cup diced cooked ham
- 1/4 cup shredded Swiss cheese
- Salt and pepper to taste
- 1 tablespoon of butter or oil

## Instructions:

- Dice cooked ham if not already.
- In a mixing bowl, beat the eggs until well combined. Next, add pepper and salt for seasoning.
- Next, heat a nonstick skillet to melt butter or oil over medium heat.
- Once the butter or oil is heated, swirl half of the beaten eggs into the skillet to ensure even distribution. Allow the eggs to cook, uncovered, for one to two minutes or until the edges are set.
- Next, sprinkle half of the diced ham and shredded Swiss

cheese over one-half of the omelet.
- Using a spatula, carefully fold the other half of the omelet over the filling to form a half-moon shape.
- Cook the omelet for another minute or two to melt the cheese.
- Repeat the process with the remaining eggs, ham, and Swiss cheese to make the second omelet.
- Serve plates of omelets immediately.

## Variations:

- **Veggie Delight:** Add diced bell peppers, onions, or mushrooms for a vegetable-packed omelet.
- **Herb Infusion:** Sprinkle chopped fresh herbs like parsley, chives, or dill over the omelet for added flavor.
- **Spicy Twist:** Add diced jalapeños or hot sauce for a spicy kick.
- **Italian Inspiration:** Incorporate diced tomatoes and basil for an Italian-inspired flavor profile.
- **Cheese Lovers' Dream:** For extra cheese, combine Swiss cheese with another favorite cheese, like cheddar or mozzarella.

(Note: Nutritional values may vary depending on the ingredients used.)

# Sunrise Fruit Parfait

- **Prep Time:** 5 minutes
- **Total Time:** 5 minutes
- **Servings:** 2
- **Calories**: Approximately 250

# Ingredients:

- 1 cup Greek yogurt
- 1/2 cup granola
- 1/2 cup mixed fresh berries (such as strawberries, blueberries, or raspberries)
- 2 tablespoons of honey or maple syrup
- Fresh mint leaves for garnish (optional)

# Instructions:

- To make this delicious parfait, use two serving glasses or bowls.
- Start by layering half the Greek yogurt between containers.
- Next, over the yogurt layer, scatter half of the granola. You can also use your favorite cereal or muesli instead of granola.
- Next, arrange half of the mixed fresh berries on the granola layer. You can use a combination of sliced strawberries, raspberries, blackberries, blueberries, or

any other berries you like. Be sure to use fresh, ripe berries for the best flavor.
- Next, repeat the layering process using the leftover Greek yogurt, granola, and mixed berries. You can adjust the amount of each ingredient according to your preference.
- Finally, to add sweetness to the parfait, drizzle some maple syrup or honey over each parfait. If you don't want to use maple syrup or honey, use agave nectar or another natural sweetener.
- Garnish with fresh mint leaves for a pop of color and freshness.
- Serve immediately and enjoy your delicious Rise and Shine Parfait!

## Variations:

- **Nutty Crunch:** For added crunch and protein, sprinkle chopped nuts—such as pecans, walnuts, or almonds—between the layers.
- **Chocolate Indulgence:** For a rich dessert, sprinkle chocolate chips or cocoa nibs between the layers.
- **Tropical Paradise:** If you want to use tropical fruits

like mango, pineapple, and kiwi, replace fruits. Replace it with mixed berries.

- **Coconut Bliss:** Layer shredded coconut with yogurt and granola for a tropical flavor profile.
- **Protein Powerhouse:** Stir protein powder into the Greek yogurt before layering to increase the protein content and make it more filling.

(Note: Nutritional values may vary depending on the specific ingredients used.)

# Ham and Egg Breakfast Roll

- **Prep Time:** 10 minutes
- **Cook Time:** 20 minutes
- **Total Time:** 30 minutes
- **Servings:** 2
- **Calories**: Approximately 300

## Ingredients:

- 2 large eggs
- 2 slices of ham
- 2 slices of bread (such as sandwich bread or French bread)
- 1/4 cup shredded cheese (cheddar, Swiss, or your choice)
- Salt and pepper to taste
- Butter or oil for frying

## Instructions:

- Preheat a skillet over medium heat. Lightly butter or oil the skillet.

- If using French bread, slice it in half lengthwise and hollow out some of the bread to make a well for the egg.

- After heating the skillet, place the ham slices and cook for one to two minutes on each side or until thoroughly cooked and lightly browned. Remove from the skillet

and set aside.
- Crack one egg into each well of the bread or directly into the skillet if not using hollowed-out bread. Season with salt and pepper.
- Cook the eggs for two to three minutes or until the yolks are still runny but the whites are mostly set.
- Top each egg with a slice of cooked ham.
- Over the ham, scatter the shredded cheese.
- If using sandwich bread, you can toast it separately in a toaster or on a skillet until golden brown.
- If using hollowed-out French bread, cover each egg and ham with the other half of the bread. If using sandwich bread, place the cooked egg, ham, and cheese between the slices of bread to form a sandwich.
- Serve immediately while warm.

## Variations:

- **Veggie Delight:** For extra flavor and nutrition, add sautéed vegetables like bell peppers, onions, and spinach to the sandwich.
- **Spicy Kick:** For a spicy twist, spread a layer of Sriracha mayo or spicy mustard on the bread before assembling

the sandwich.

- **Cheese Lovers':** For a cheese feast, try mozzarella, pepperjack, or provolone.
- **Breakfast Burrito Style:** To make a breakfast burrito, wrap the cooked egg, ham, and cheese in a large tortilla instead of using bread.
- **Italian Influence:** Add slices of tomato and basil leaves to the sandwich for an Italian-inspired flavor profile.

(Note: Nutritional values may vary depending on the ingredients used.)

# Italian Egg Meringue

- **Prep Time:** 10 minutes
- **Cook Time:** 10 minutes
- **Total Time:** 20 minutes
- **Servings:** 2
- **Calories**: approximately 120

## Ingredients:

- 4 large eggs
- 1/4 cup grated Parmesan cheese
- 1/4 cup diced tomatoes
- 1 tablespoon chopped fresh basil
- Salt and pepper to taste
- Optional: sliced bread or toast for serving.

## Instructions:

- First, preheat oven to 375°F (190°C). Next, use parchment paper to cover a baking sheet.
- Now crack the egg gently, separate the yolks and egg whites, and place them in separate bowls.
- Using a stand or hand mixer, beat the egg whites until stiff peaks form.
- Gently fold the grated Parmesan cheese, diced tomatoes, and chopped fresh basil into the whipped egg whites—season with salt and pepper to taste.

- Divide the egg white mixture into 4 equal portions on the prepared baking sheet, shaping each portion into a cloud-like mound with a well in the center.
- After preheating the oven, bake the egg whites for 3–5 minutes until the edges turn golden.
- With care, put one egg yolk in the middle of each cloud.
- Return the baking sheet to the oven and bake for 3-5 minutes until the egg yolks are set to your desired level of doneness.
- Remove from the oven and immediately serve the Italian Cloud Eggs, either as they are or with sliced bread or toast for dipping.

## Variations:

- **Mediterranean Twist:** Add diced olives, sun-dried tomatoes, and feta cheese to the egg white mixture for a Mediterranean flavor profile.
- **Spicy Kick:** Stir in a pinch of red pepper flakes or add a dollop of zesty marinara sauce on top of each cloud for some heat.
- **Cheese Lover's Dream:** Sprinkle additional shredded mozzarella or fontina cheese over the egg whites before

baking for extra cheesiness.

- **Herb Infusion:** Add finely chopped parsley, oregano, or thyme for flavor and freshness.
- **Vegetarian Option:** Omit the diced tomatoes and add sautéed mushrooms, spinach, and onions for a vegetarian variation.

(Note: Nutritional values may vary depending on the ingredients used.)

# Cinnamon Apple Oats in a Jar

- **Prep Time:** 5 minutes
- **Total Time:** 8 hours (overnight)
- **Servings:** 2
- **Calories**: Approximately 250

## Ingredients:

- 1 cup rolled oats
- 1 cup milk (dairy or plant-based)
- 1 medium apple, grated or finely chopped
- 2 tablespoons of honey or maple syrup
- 1/2 teaspoon ground cinnamon
- **Optional toppings:** chopped nuts, additional apple slices, or a drizzle of honey.

## Instructions:

- In a mixing bowl or jar, mix the rolled oats, milk, grated apple, honey or maple syrup, and ground cinnamon. Stir well to combine.
- Cover and refrigerate for 8 hours or overnight to soften and absorb the oats.
- Before serving, mix the overnight oats well.
- If desired, top with chopped nuts, additional apple slices, or a drizzle of honey for extra flavor and texture.
- Serve the apple-cinnamon overnight oats from the

refrigerator for a delicious and nutritious breakfast.

## Variations:

- **Nutty Crunch:** Stir chopped nuts like almonds, walnuts, or pecans for added protein and crunch.
- **Maple-Pecan Flavor:** Replace the honey with maple syrup and add a handful of chopped pecans for a delightful maple-pecan twist.
- **Apple Pie Inspired:** Mix in a tablespoon of unsweetened applesauce, a pinch of nutmeg, and cloves for a flavor reminiscent of apple pie.
- **Berries Galore:** Add a handful of fresh or frozen berries like blueberries, raspberries, or strawberries for a burst of fruity goodness.
- **Coconut Delight:** Sprinkle shredded coconut on the overnight oats for a tropical flavor and added texture.

(Note: Nutritional values may vary depending on specific ingredients and toppings.)

# Breakfast Caprese Egg Sandwich

- **Prep Time:** 5 minutes
- **Cook Time:** 5 minutes
- **Total Time:** 10 minutes
- **Servings:** 2
- **Calories**: Approximately 450

## Ingredients:

- 4 slices of bread (whole wheat, multigrain, or your choice)
- 2 tablespoons of pesto sauce
- 2 slices of mozzarella cheese
- 2 large eggs
- Salt and pepper to taste
- Optional: sliced tomato, avocado, or spinach leaves for extra flavor.

## Instructions:

- First, toast the bread slices until golden brown and crispy.
- After toasted, apply pesto sauce over one side.
- Next, crack an egg in a skillet over medium heat and cook it to your desired doneness. Add salt and pepper to taste.
- Add mozzarella cheese to one pesto-covered bread slice. Place the cooked egg.

- Add sliced tomato, avocado, or spinach leaves for extra flavor if desired.
- Slide the other pesto-covered bread on top to finish the sandwich.
- Serve the pesto, mozzarella, and egg breakfast sandwich immediately while warm.

## Variations:

- **Bacon Bliss:** Add crispy bacon slices to the sandwich for a savory bacon and egg combo.
- **Caprese Twist:** Layer sliced tomato, fresh basil leaves, and mozzarella cheese for a Caprese-inspired flavor.
- **Avocado Addition:** Mash avocado on one side of the bread for a creamy and nutritious addition.
- **Spinach Surprise:** Add a handful of fresh spinach leaves to the sandwich for extra greens and vitamins.
- **Red Pepper Relish:** Spread roasted red pepper relish on one side of the bread for a sweet and tangy kick.

(Note: Nutritional values may vary depending on the ingredients used.)

# Morning Sweet Potato Delight

- **Prep Time:** 10 minutes
- **Cook Time:** 40 minutes
- **Total Time:** 50 minutes
- **Servings:** 2
- **Calories:** Approximately 300

## Ingredients:

- 4 medium sweet potatoes
- 1/2 cup fat-free coconut Greek yogurt
- 1 medium apple, chopped
- 2 tablespoons of maple syrup
- 1/4 cup toasted, unsweetened coconut flakes

## Instructions:

- First, preheat your oven to 400°F (200°C).
- Next, scrubbing the sweet potatoes clean under running water is essential to remove dirt or debris. After cleaning, dry with a paper towel.
- Using a fork, poke the potatoes a few times. This step is crucial, as it allows steam to escape while baking, preventing it from bursting open in the oven.
- After that, bake it in the oven for 40 minutes.
- Prepare the topping while baking the sweet potatoes. First, chop up an apple into small pieces. In a small

bowl, mix chopped apple, maple syrup, and toasted unsweetened coconut flakes.
- Seasoned potatoes are ready. Slice them lengthwise.
- Spread coconut Greek yogurt evenly on each sweet potato.
- Top with the prepared apple, maple syrup, and coconut topping mixture.
- While hot, immediately serve the breakfast sweet potatoes for a delightful and flavorful dish.

## Variations:

- **Nutty Crunch:** Add chopped pecans or almonds for protein and crunch.
- **Cinnamon Spice:** Mix a teaspoon of cinnamon into the coconut Greek yogurt for a warm, spicy flavor.
- **Berry Blast:** Replace apples with strawberries, blueberries, and raspberries for fruity sweetness.
- **Savory Twist:** Skip the sweet toppings and stuff the sweet potatoes with scrambled eggs, spinach, and feta cheese for a delicious breakfast.
- **Protein Power:** Add cooked quinoa, diced chicken, and a drizzle of tahini for an extra protein boost.

(Note: Nutritional values may vary depending on specific ingredients and portion sizes.)

# Fruity Waffle Parfaits

- **Prep Time:** 10 minutes
- **Cook Time:** 10 minutes
- **Total Time:** 20 minutes
- **Servings:** 2
- **Calories**: Approximately 250

## Ingredients:

- 2 frozen waffles, toasted according to package instructions
- 1 cup Greek yogurt
- 1 cup mixed fresh fruits (such as strawberries, blueberries, and bananas), chopped
- 2 tablespoons of honey or maple syrup
- 1/4 cup granola or chopped nuts (optional)

## Instructions:

- Toast frozen waffles as directed on the package until crispy and golden brown.
- In serving glasses or bowls, crumble one toasted waffle at the bottom to form the first layer.
- On top of the waffle crumbs, spread a layer of Greek yogurt.
- Arrange a portion of the mixed fresh fruits on the yogurt layer.
- Drizzle with honey or maple syrup.

- Continue layering by adding more crumbled waffles, Greek yogurt, a mixture of fresh fruit, and either honey or maple syrup.
- Add crunch and texture with granola or chopped nuts on top.
- Serve the fruity waffle parfaits immediately and enjoy a delightful breakfast or snack.

## Variations:

- **Chocolate Lover's Delight:** For a sweet treat, sprinkle chocolate chips or chocolate syrup between the layers.
- **Tropical Paradise:** Add fruits like mango, pineapple, and kiwi for a refreshing twist.
- **Nutty Crunch:** Enhance your dish with sliced almonds, walnuts, or pecans to add protein and crunchiness.
- **Berry blast:** Use berries like raspberries, blackberries, and blueberries.
- **Coconut Dream:** Sprinkle shredded coconut over each layer for a tropical flair.

(Note: Nutritional values may vary depending on specific ingredients and portion sizes.)

# Banana Flip Pancakes

- **Prep Time:** 5 minutes
- **Cook Time:** 10 minutes
- **Total Time:** 15 minutes
- **Servings:** 2
- **Calories**: Approximately 200

## Ingredients:

- 1 large, ripe banana
- 2 large eggs

## Instructions:

- Peel and mash the ripe banana in a mixing bowl until smooth.
- Now, crack the eggs in the bowl.
- Use a fork or whisk to thoroughly mix the mashed banana and eggs until well combined and smooth.
- Over medium heat, preheat a nonstick skillet or griddle.
- Apply a small cooking spray or butter to grease the skillet lightly.
- Pour 1/4 cup of batter per pancake onto the skillet in small circles.
- Cook pancakes until bubbles form on one side for 2-3 minutes.

- Flip the pancakes and cook on the other side for 1-2 minutes until golden brown and cooked through.
- Transfer the cooked pancakes to serving plates.
- Serve the two-ingredient banana pancakes warm, optionally topped with maple syrup, honey, fresh fruit, or your favorite pancake toppings.

## Variations:

- **Cinnamon Spice:** Add a pinch of ground cinnamon to the batter for flavor.
- **Nutty Crunch:** Stir chopped nuts like walnuts or pecans for added texture.
- **Chocolate Indulgence:** Sprinkle chocolate chips into the batter for a decadent treat.
- **Berry Burst:** Add fresh or frozen blueberries or raspberries for fruity bursts.
- **Coconut Delight:** Add shredded coconut for a tropical touch.

(Note: Nutritional values may vary depending on the specific ingredients used and any toppings added.)

# Waffle Breakfast Sandwich

- **Prep Time:** 5 minutes
- **Cook Time:** 5 minutes
- **Total Time:** 10 minutes
- **Servings:** 2
- **Calories**: Approximately 400

## Ingredients:

- 4 frozen waffles, toasted according to package instructions
- 4 slices of cooked bacon or ham
- 2 cooked eggs (sunny-side-up, over-easy, or scrambled)
- 2 slices of cheese (cheddar, Swiss, or your choice)
- Maple syrup or honey for drizzling (optional)

## Instructions:

- First, toast the frozen waffles in the toaster oven for 2-3 minutes on the lowest setting.
- Make sure the waffles turn golden brown and crispy.
- Next, fry bacon or ham slices in a skillet over medium heat until crispy.
- Next, in the same skillet, cook eggs sunny-side-up, over-easy, or scrambled.
- Now Place two slices of cooked bacon or ham on two toasted waffles.

- Place an egg on top of the bacon or ham on each waffle.
- Place a slice of cheese on top of each egg.
- Top with the remaining two toasted waffles to complete the sandwiches.
- Serve immediately for a delicious breakfast or brunch.
- Optionally, drizzle with maple syrup or honey for a touch of sweetness.

## Variations:

- **Vegetarian Option:** Replace bacon and ham with sliced avocado, tomato, and spinach.
- **Sweet and Savory:** Spread a thin layer of peanut butter or almond butter on one side of the waffle before assembling for a sweet and savory combination.
- **Spicy Kick:** Add a dash of hot sauce or sriracha to the egg for an extra kick of flavor.
- **Southwestern Twist:** Add sliced jalapeños, black beans, salsa, and a dollop of sour cream for a Southwestern-inspired waffle sandwich.
- **Breakfast Burrito Style:** Add cooked breakfast potatoes, salsa, and a sprinkle of shredded cheese for a burrito-inspired waffle sandwich.

# Salsa-Infused Scramble

- **Prep Time:** 5 minutes
- **Cook Time:** 5 minutes
- **Total Time:** 10 minutes
- **Servings:** 2
- **Calories**: Approximately 150

## Ingredients:

- 4 large eggs
- 1/4 cup salsa (homemade or store-bought)
- 2 tablespoons of milk (dairy or plant-based)
- Salt and pepper to taste
- 2 corn tortillas, warmed
- 1 tablespoon chopped fresh cilantro (optional, for garnish)
- Optional: shredded cheese, diced avocado, or sour cream for serving.

## Instructions:

- First, crack eggs into a medium bowl. Then, add 1/4 cup of your favorite salsa and 2 tablespoons of milk. Season with salt and pepper and wick until well combined and slightly frothy.
- Next, place a nonstick skillet on medium heat. Once the skillet is hot, pour the egg mixture into the skillet. Cook

the eggs for 1-2 minutes. Stir the eggs gently until scrambled and cook to your liking.
- After cooking, arrange the scrambled eggs into corn tortillas.
- Top with chopped fresh cilantro and additional toppings such as shredded cheese, diced avocado, or sour cream if desired.
- Serve the scrambled eggs with salsa and enjoy a delicious breakfast or brunch.

## Variations:

- **Spicy Kick:** Use a spicy salsa or add a dash of hot sauce to the eggs for extra heat.
- **Vegetarian Delight:** Add diced bell peppers, onions, or mushrooms to the eggs for flavor and texture.
- **Tex-Mex Twist:** Scrambled eggs on warm tortillas make delicious breakfast tacos.
- **Protein Boost:** Stir in cooked black beans or tofu for added protein and substance.
- **Cheesy Goodness:** Sprinkle shredded cheese over the scrambled eggs while they cook for extra cheesy flavor.

# Southern Egg Sandwich

- **Prep Time:** 5 minutes
- **Cook Time:** 5 minutes
- **Total Time:** 10 minutes
- **Servings:** 2
- **Calories**: Approximately 400

## Ingredients:

- 4 slices of bread (your choice of bread, such as white, whole wheat, or sourdough)
- 4 large eggs
- 1/2 cup pimiento cheese spread
- 2 tablespoons of butter
- Salt and pepper to taste
- Optional: sliced tomato, lettuce, or cooked bacon for serving.

## Instructions:

- In a non-stick skillet, melt 1 tablespoon of butter over medium heat.
- Next, crack eggs into a skillet and cook them to your desired level of doneness, whether sunny-side-up, over-easy, or scrambled. Then, season with salt and pepper to your taste.
- Toast two slices of bread until golden brown while the eggs cook. After toasting the bread, generously spread

pimiento cheese on each slice.
- After cooking, place the eggs on top of the pimiento cheese.
- If desired, add sliced tomato, lettuce, or cooked bacon on top of the eggs.
- Place the remaining slices of toast on top of the sandwich halves and slice them diagonally.
- Enjoy your delicious Pimiento Cheese and Egg Sandwiches!

## Variations:

- **Spicy Kick:** To add some spicy flavor to the eggs, top them with red pepper flakes or a few dashes of hot sauce.
- **Avocado Addition:** Spread mashed avocado on one side of the bread before assembling the sandwich for extra creaminess and flavor.
- **Pickled Twist:** Add a few slices of pickled jalapeños or banana peppers for a tangy and spicy kick.
- **Bacon Lover's Delight:** Add crispy cooked bacon strips to the sandwich for an extra layer of flavor and texture.
- **Herb Infusion:** Mix chopped fresh herbs like parsley, chives, or dill into the pimiento cheese for a burst of freshness.

# Bagel Bonanza Banana

- **Prep Time:** 5 minutes
- **Cook Time:** 5 minutes
- **Total Time:** 10 minutes
- **Servings:** 2
- **Calories**: Approximately 350

## Ingredients:

- 2 bagels, sliced and toasted
- 1 ripe banana, sliced
- 2 tablespoons of creamy peanut butter
- 2 tablespoons honey or maple syrup (optional)
- Optional toppings: sliced strawberries, blueberries, chopped nuts, or chocolate chips.

## Instructions:

- First, slice the bagels in half and toast until golden brown.
- Apply 1 tablespoon of creamy peanut butter to each half of the toasted bagels.
- Place sliced bananas on top of peanut butter on each bagel half.
- Drizzle 1 tablespoon of honey over the banana slices on each bagel half.
- If desired, add toppings such as sliced strawberries,

blueberries, chopped nuts, or chocolate chips on top of the bananas and honey.

- Enjoy it as a tasty breakfast or snack now!

# Variations:

- **Chocolate Delight:** Sprinkle chocolate chips or cocoa nibs over the banana slices for a chocolatey twist.
- **Nutty Crunch:** Add chopped nuts (almonds, walnuts, or pecans) to the top for a crunch and an extra protein boost.
- **Berry Blast:** Add sliced raspberries, blueberries, or strawberries on top for a juicy taste.
- **Coconut Paradise:** Sprinkle shredded coconut over the bananas and honey for a tropical flair.
- **Cinnamon Spice:** To add a cozy and fragrant taste to the banana slices, sprinkle them with ground cinnamon.

# Creamy Herb Omelette

- **Prep Time:** 5 minutes
- **Cook Time:** 5 minutes
- **Total Time:** 10 minutes
- **Servings:** 2
- **Calories**: Approximately 250

## Ingredients:

- 4 large eggs
- 4 tablespoons cream cheese, softened
- 2 tablespoons chopped fresh chives
- Salt and pepper, to taste
- 2 tablespoons of butter or cooking oil

## Instructions:

- Start by cracking eggs into a small bowl and beating them well until thoroughly mixed.
- Then, chop the fresh chives into small pieces, removing the tough stems.
- Next, take another bowl and mix the softened cream cheese and chopped chives until they are well combined. Add salt and pepper to the mixture based on your preference.
- Now, take a non-stick skillet and heat 1 tablespoon of butter or cooking oil over medium heat until it is melted

and hot.
- Pour half of the whisked eggs into the skillet and cook until the edges are set about 1 minute.
- Once the edges start to set, spoon half of the cream cheese and chive mixture onto one half of the omelet; with caution, fold the remaining omelet over the mixture to form a half-moon. For the second omelet, follow the same procedure.
- Continue cooking the omelet until the eggs are set and the cheese melts.
- Finally, slide each omelet onto a plate and serve immediately. Enjoy your tasty and nutritious breakfast!

## Variations:

- **Add Vegetables:** To add more taste and nutrients to your omelet, add sautéed bell peppers, onions, spinach, or mushrooms.
- **Cheese Options:** Experiment with different types of cheese, such as cheddar, feta, or Swiss, to customize the flavor of your omelet.
- **Herb Substitutions:** You can substitute chives for other herbs like parsley, dill, or basil based on your

preference and availability.

- **Spice it up:** For a spicy flavor, add a pinch of paprika, cayenne pepper, or red pepper flakes.
- **Protein Boost:** Incorporate cooked bacon, ham, sausage, or smoked salmon to add protein and enhance the taste of your omelet.

(Note: Nutritional values may vary depending on specific ingredients and portion sizes.)

# Express Spinach Omelette

- **Prep Time:** 5 minutes
- **Cook Time:** 5 minutes
- **Total Time:** 10 minutes
- **Servings:** 2
- **Calories**: Approximately 300

## Ingredients:

- 4 large eggs
- 2 cups fresh spinach leaves, roughly chopped
- 1/2 cup shredded cheese (cheddar, mozzarella, or your choice)
- 2 tablespoons of olive oil or butter
- Salt and pepper to taste

## Instructions:

- Wash the fresh spinach leaves thoroughly and roughly chop them.
- In a bowl, beat eggs thoroughly with a fork or whisker. Add salt and pepper to taste and mix thoroughly.
- Next, place a non-stick skillet over medium heat and add either butter or olive oil.
- Once the skillet is heated up, add the finely chopped spinach to it. sauté the spinach for 1-2 minutes until it wilts and becomes tender.

- Pour the beaten eggs over the sautéed spinach.
- Allow the eggs to cook undisturbed for about 2–3 minutes until the edges start to set.
- Then, sprinkle the shredded cheese evenly over one-half of each omelet.
- Using a spatula, carefully fold the other half of each omelet over the cheese.
- Cook for another 1-2 minutes until the cheese melts and the omelets are cooked.
- Slide each spinach omelet onto a plate and serve hot.

## Variations:

- **Mushroom Medley:** Add sliced mushrooms to the spinach while sautéing for extra flavor and texture.
- **Tomato Tango:** Add diced tomatoes to the omelets before folding for a juicy and refreshing twist.
- **Herb Infusion:** Sprinkle chopped fresh herbs such as parsley, chives, or dill over the omelets for added freshness.
- **Feta Fusion:** Replace the shredded cheese with crumbled feta cheese for a tangy and savory flavor.
- **Onion Obsession:** Add thinly sliced onions to the

spinach while sautéing for extra depth of flavor.

(Note: Nutritional values may vary depending on specific ingredients and portion sizes.)

# Egg Provolone Panini

- **Prep Time:** 5 minutes
- **Cook Time:** 5 minutes
- **Total Time:** 10 minutes
- **Servings:** 2
- **Calories**: Approximately 450

## Ingredients:

- 4 slices of bread (your choice of bread, such as white, whole wheat, or sourdough)
- 4 large eggs
- 4 slices of salami
- 2 slices of provolone cheese
- 2 tablespoons of butter
- Salt and pepper to taste

## Instructions:

- In a non-stick skillet, melt 1 tablespoon of butter over medium heat.
- Next, crack eggs into a skillet and cook until desired level of doneness is reached, whether sunny-side-up, over-easy, or scrambled. Next, add salt and pepper to taste.
- While eggs cook, heat another skillet over medium heat. and Cook the salami slices in the skillet for one to two minutes on each side, or until they are crispy and lightly

browned.
- Next, toast the bread slices until golden brown.
- Place a slice of provolone cheese on two of the toasted bread slices.
- Top each slice of cheese with two slices of cooked salami.
- On top of the salami, arrange the eggs. To assemble the sandwiches, place the remaining toasted bread slices on the eggs to form sandwiches.
- Using a sharp knife, cut each sandwich in half diagonally after they have been assembled.

## Variations:

- **Herb Infusion:** Add chopped fresh herbs like basil or parsley to the eggs while they are cooking for extra flavor.
- **Spicy Kick:** Spread a thin layer of spicy mustard or Sriracha mayo on the bread slices before assembling the sandwiches for some heat.
- **Veggie Boost:** Add sliced tomatoes, avocado, or lettuce to the sandwiches for a refreshing twist.
- **Cheesy Upgrade:** Add additional slices of provolone

cheese or swap it for your favorite cheese for extra cheesiness.

(Note: Nutritional values may vary depending on specific ingredients used and portion sizes.)

# Smoky Salmon Breakfast Scramble

- **Prep Time:** 5 minutes
- **Cook Time:** 5 minutes
- **Total Time:** 10 minutes
- **Servings:** 2
- **Calories**: Approximately 200

## Ingredients:

- 4 large eggs
- 2 ounces smoked salmon, chopped
- 2 tablespoons of milk (dairy or plant-based)
- Salt and pepper to taste
- 1 tablespoon chopped fresh chives (optional, for garnish)
- Butter or cooking oil for cooking

## Instructions:

- Crack the eggs and whisk them with the milk in a mixing bowl. Use a fork or whisk to mix the eggs.
- Next, heat the skillet on medium heat and add a small quantity of butter or cooking oil.
- Pour the whisked eggs into the skillet and let them cook, stirring gently with a spatula, until they begin to set.
- As the eggs solidify, toss the chopped smoked salmon into the skillet. Keep stirring the eggs until they reach

your desired texture, and the smoked salmon is cooked.
- Season the scrambled eggs with salt and pepper according to your preference.
- Top the scrambled eggs with chopped, fresh chives for color and flavor if desired.
- Serve the smoked salmon scrambled eggs hot, accompanied by toast, bagels, or your favorite breakfast sides.

## Variations:

- **Creamy Texture:** Add a dollop of cream cheese or sour cream to the eggs while cooking for a creamier texture.
- **Herbal Infusion:** Toss some finely chopped fresh parsley or dill for flavor.
- **Vegetable Medley:** Add diced onions, bell peppers, or spinach to the eggs for extra flavor and nutrients.
- **Cheese Lover's Delight:** For added richness, sprinkle shredded cheese (such as cheddar or Gruyere) over the eggs before serving.
- **Spicy Kick:** Sprinkle sauce or red pepper flakes on eggs for a kick.

## Oatmeal Banana Hotcakes

- **Prep Time**: 10 minutes
- **Cook Time**: 10 minutes
- **Total Time:** 20 minutes
- **Servings:** 2
- **Calories:** Approximately 200

## Ingredients:

- 1 ripe banana
- 1/2 cup rolled oats
- 1/4 cup milk (dairy or plant-based)
- 1 egg
- Pinch of salt

## Instructions:

- First, mash the ripe banana in a mixing bowl until smooth.
- Add the rolled oats to the mashed banana and stir them until nicely mixed.
- In another bowl, add the egg and milk, stirring to mix thoroughly. To ensure egg distribution in the batter, beat it thoroughly.
- Once the wet ingredients are mixed, pour them into the

bowl with the mashed banana and oats. Stir well to combine ingredients into a thick batter.
- Next, heat a griddle or non-stick skillet on medium.
- Now, grease the pan lightly with butter or oil. Pour 1/4 cup of batter and spread the batter with a spoon or spatula. Let the pancake cook on each side for two to three minutes until bubbles appear on the surface.
- Now flip and cook for another 1-2 minutes or until golden brown. The second side will cook faster than the first, so keep an eye on the pancakes to ensure they don't burn.
- Serve pancakes with bananas, berries, maple syrup, yogurt, or nut butter.
- Add honey or whipped cream for a decadent treat. Enjoy!

## Variations:

- **Chocolate Chip Delight:** Add chocolate chips to the mix for extra decadence.
- **Berry Blast:** Fold fresh or frozen berries, such as blueberries, raspberries, or strawberries, into the batter before cooking.

- **Coconut Paradise:** Sprinkle shredded coconut onto the pancakes while they cook for a tropical twist.
- **Pumpkin Spice Flair:** Replace the banana with pumpkin puree and add pumpkin pie spice for a seasonal variation.

(Note: Nutritional values may vary depending on the ingredients used.)

# Rhubarb Yogurt Parfait

- **Prep Time:** 10 minutes
- **Cook Time:** 15 minutes
- **Total Time:** 25 minutes
- **Servings:** 2
- **Calories**: Approximately 200

## Ingredients:

- 2 cups rhubarb, chopped into small pieces
- 1/4 cup sugar
- 1/4 cup of water
- 1 cup Greek yogurt
- 1/4 cup sliced almonds
- Honey or maple syrup for drizzling (optional)

## Instructions:

- First, take the rhubarb stalks and wash them thoroughly under running water.
- Now, take a saucepan and add the chopped rhubarb, some sugar, and water.
- Place the saucepan on medium heat on the stove. Start stirring the mixture occasionally so the sugar dissolves and the rhubarb pieces break down and become tender. Keep stirring until the rhubarb is cooked, usually 10–15 minutes.

- After cooking the rhubarb, taste the mixture and add sugar if needed.
- Remove the rhubarb and let it cool slightly.
- Divide the Greek yogurt evenly between two serving bowls.
- Spoon the warm rhubarb compote over the yogurt.
- Sprinkle sliced almonds on top of the rhubarb compote.
- If desired, add some extra sweetness by drizzling honey or maple syrup on top.
- Serve the rhubarb compote with yogurt and almonds immediately.

## Variations:

- **Granola Crunch:** Add a crunchy texture by sprinkling granola on top of the yogurt and rhubarb compote.
- **Zest from Citrus:** Sprinkle some zest from lemons or oranges over the dish.
- **Coconut Flakes:** Add toasted coconut flakes to the yogurt and rhubarb for a tropical touch.
- **Fresh Mint:** Add some fresh mint leaves as a garnish to your dish for a refreshing aroma and taste.
- **Chia Seeds:** Boost the nutritional value by sprinkling

chia seeds over the yogurt for added fiber and omega-3 fatty acids.

(Note: Nutritional values may vary depending on specific ingredients and portion sizes.)

# Peanut Butter Banana Breakfast Delight

- **Prep Time:** 5 minutes
- **Servings:** 2
- **Calories**: 380

## Ingredients:

- 2 ripe bananas, frozen
- 1 cup of plain Greek yogurt
- 4 tablespoons of peanut butter
- 1/2 cup almond milk (or any milk of your choice)
- Toppings of your choice (such as sliced banana, granola, chia seeds, shredded coconut, or a drizzle of honey)

## Instructions:

- First take 2 ripe bananas, peel them, and slice them into chunks of about 1-2 inches.
- Arrange the banana chunks on a baking sheet covered with parchment. Then, freeze the sheet for 2 hours or overnight to freeze the bananas.
- Next, remove the frozen banana chunks from the freezer and place them in a blender. Add 1/2 cup of Greek yogurt, 1/4 cup of peanut butter, and 1/2 cup of almond milk to the blender.

- Next, blend until smooth and creamy, scraping down the blender sides, and divide between two bowls. You can use a spatula to scrape all the mixture from the blender.
- For the garnish, you can use sliced banana, granola, chia seeds, shredded coconut, or a drizzle of honey. Feel free to get creative and try different topping combinations!
- Finally, serve the smoothie bowls immediately with a spoon and enjoy the delicious and healthy treat!

## Variations:

- **Chocolate Lover's Delight:** Stir in two tablespoons of cocoa powder to give the smoothie base a chocolaty twist. Toss in some chocolate chips for an extra treat.
- **Berry Blast:** Blend 1/2 cup of mixed berries (strawberries, blueberries, or raspberries) with the smoothie base for a fruity flavor. Top with additional fresh berries for garnish.
- **Green Goddess:** Add a handful of spinach or kale to the smoothie base for an extra green boost. Top with sliced kiwi or pineapple for a tropical touch.

- **Protein Powerhouse:** Add a scoop of your favorite protein powder to the smoothie base for added protein. Top with sliced almonds or hemp seeds for extra protein and crunch.
- **Tropical Paradise:** Blend 1/2 cup of frozen pineapple chunks with the smoothie base for a tropical twist. Top with toasted coconut flakes and a squeeze of lime juice for a refreshing flavor.

(Note: Nutritional values may vary depending on specific ingredients and serving sizes.)

# Egg and Toast Soldiers

- **Prep Time:** 5 minutes
- **Cook Time:** 6 minutes
- **Total Time:** 11 minutes
- **Servings:** 2
- **Calories**: approximately 220

## Ingredients:

- 4 large eggs
- 4 slices of bread, toasted
- Butter for spreading
- Salt and pepper to taste
- Fresh chives or parsley for garnish (optional)

## Instructions:

- Gently boil water in a pot over medium heat.
- Using a slotted spoon, carefully drop the eggs into the boiling water.
- For soft-boiled eggs with a slightly runny yolk, boil for 2-3 minutes.
- While the eggs are boiling, put the slices of bread in the oven and toast them until golden brown.
- Cut the toasted bread into about 1-inch-wide strips to serve as "soldiers."
- Using a slotted spoon, carefully remove the eggs from

the boiling water and place them in an egg cup or small bowl.
- Use a knife to carefully crack the tops of the eggs and remove the shells.
- Place the soft-boiled eggs in egg cups or small bowls.
- Season the eggs with salt and pepper, to taste.
- Spread butter on the toasted soldiers.
- Serve the soft-boiled eggs with the buttered soldiers for dipping.
- Serving with chopped fresh chives or parsley is optional.

## Variations:

- **Cheesy Soldiers:** Sprinkle grated cheese over the buttered soldiers and melt under the broiler for a delicious cheesy twist.
- **Herb Infusion:** Mix chopped fresh herbs like dill, parsley, or chives into the butter for extra flavor.
- **Bacon Wrapped:** Serve crispy bacon strips alongside the soldiers for a savory addition.
- **Avocado Smash:** Spread mashed avocado on the sandwiches instead of butter for a creamy and nutritious

option.

- **Spiced Up:** Sprinkle paprika, chili flakes, or your favorite spice blend over the eggs for added flavor.

(Note: Nutritional values may vary depending on specific ingredients and portion sizes.)

# Breakfast Bread Cup

- **Prep Time:** 10 minutes
- **Cook Time:** 20 minutes
- **Total Time:** 30 minutes
- **Servings:** 2
- **Calories**: Approximately 300

## Ingredients:

- 2 small bread rolls (such as sourdough or whole grain)
- 2 large eggs
- 1/4 cup shredded cheese (cheddar, mozzarella, or your choice)
- 2 slices of cooked bacon or sausage (optional)
- Salt and pepper to taste
- Fresh herbs for garnish (optional)

## Instructions:

- Preheat your oven to 350°F (175°C).
- Use a knife to cut off the top portion of each bread roll.
- Gently hollow out the center of each roll, forming a "bowl" with a thick border around the edges."
- Next, crack one egg into each bread bowl and season with salt and pepper to taste.
- Sprinkle shredded cheese over the eggs.
- If using, top cheese with cooked bacon or sausage.
- On a baking sheet, arrange the filled bread bowls.

- Place it in a preheated oven for 20 minutes or until the yolks are cooked to your preference.
- Once baked, remove the bread bowls from the oven.
- If desired, garnish with fresh herbs.
- Serve hot and enjoy breakfast bread bowls!

## Variations:

- **Vegetarian Option:** Add sautéed veggies like bell peppers, onions, and spinach in place of the bacon or sausage.
- **Spicy Kick:** Sprinkle red pepper flakes or drizzle hot sauce over the eggs before baking for a spicy twist.
- **Mexican-Inspired:** Top with salsa, avocado slices, and a dollop of sour cream after baking for a Tex-Mex flair.
- **Mushroom & Swiss:** Sauté sliced mushrooms and onions until tender, then mix with shredded Swiss cheese to fill the bread bowls.
- **Caprese Style:** To achieve the traditional Caprese flavor, add sliced tomatoes, mozzarella cheese, and fresh basil leaves.

(Note: Nutritional values may vary depending on the specific ingredients used.)

# Sausage Cheese Breakfast Wrap

- **Prep Time:** 10 minutes
- **Cook Time:** 10 minutes
- **Total Time:** 20 minutes
- **Servings:** 2
- **Calories**: 470

## Ingredients:

- 4 large eggs
- 2 sausage links, cooked and sliced
- 1/2 cup shredded cheese (cheddar, Monterey Jack, or your choice)
- 2 large flour tortillas
- Salt and pepper to taste
- Salsa, avocado slices, or sour cream for serving (optional)

## Instructions:

- Whisk together the eggs in a bowl and season with salt and pepper.
- Next, preheat a nonstick skillet to medium heat and coat it with olive oil.
- After it is properly heated, Pour the whisked eggs into the skillet and let them cook, stirring occasionally, until they become scrambled and cooked.
- Next, heat the flour tortillas in the microwave or skillet

and soften them for a few seconds.
- Spread scrambled eggs in the center of each tortilla.
- Arrange the cooked sausage slices on top of the eggs in each tortilla.
- Sprinkle shredded cheese over the sausage and eggs.
- Fold the sides of the tortilla over the filling, ensuring they overlap. Tightly roll the tortilla from the bottom up, enclosing the filling completely, to form a burrito.
- Serve the breakfast burritos immediately, with salsa, avocado slices, or sour cream on the side if desired.

## Variations:

- **Veggie Lovers:** For a vegetarian option, add sautéed bell peppers, onions, and spinach to the scrambled eggs.
- **Southwest Flavor:** Mix in some black beans, diced tomatoes, and a sprinkle of chili powder for a Tex-Mex twist.
- **Healthy Swap:** Try whole wheat or spinach tortillas for more nutrients and fiber.
- **Extra Heat:** Add sliced jalapeños or a dash of hot sauce to spice up your breakfast burrito.
- **Protein Boost:** Add cooked bacon or ham and the

sausage for extra protein.

(Note: Nutritional values are approximate and may vary depending on specific ingredients and portion sizes.)

# Ricotta Bean Bruschetta Toast

- **Prep Time:** 5 minutes
- **Cook Time:** 5 minutes
- **Total Time:** 10 minutes
- **Servings:** 2
- **Calories**: Approximately 300

## Ingredients:

- 4 slices of bread (such as sourdough or whole grain), toasted
- 1 can (15 ounces) cannellini beans, drained and rinsed
- 1/2 cup ricotta cheese
- 1 tablespoon chopped fresh herbs (such as parsley, thyme, or basil)
- Salt and pepper to taste
- Olive oil for drizzling

## Instructions:

- Toast the bread slices until they turn golden brown.
- Mix the ricotta cheese and chopped fresh herbs in a small bowl. Season with salt and pepper to taste.
- In another bowl, lightly mash the cannellini beans with a fork. Season with salt and pepper, if desired.
- Spread a generous layer of herbed ricotta on each slice of toasted bread.
- Spoon the mashed cannellini beans over the herbed

ricotta layer.
- Over each toast, drizzle a little olive oil.
- If desired, add chopped fresh herbs to the cannellini bean and herb ricotta toast.
- Serve immediately for a healthy breakfast or snack.

## Variations:

- **Tomato Twist:** Add sliced cherry or sun-dried tomatoes on top of the ricotta for freshness.
- **Avocado:** Add ripe avocado slices to toast for creaminess and flavor.
- **Poached Egg Perfection:** Serve a poached egg on top of each toast for a protein-packed meal.
- **Spicy Kick:** Sprinkle red pepper flakes or drizzle hot sauce over the toast for a spicy twist.
- **Balsamic Glaze:** Drizzle some balsamic glaze over the toast for a tart and sweet finish.

(Note: Nutritional values may vary depending on specific ingredients and portion sizes.)

# Fruity Nut Oatmeal Mix

- **Prep Time:** 5 minutes
- **Cook Time:** 5 minutes
- **Total Time:** 10 minutes
- **Servings:** 2
- **Calories**: Approximately 300

## Ingredients:

- 1 cup rolled oats
- 2 cups water or milk (dairy or plant-based)
- 1 ripe banana, sliced
- 1/4 cup chopped nuts (such as almonds, walnuts, or pecans)
- 1/4 cup dried fruit (such as raisins, cranberries, or chopped apricots)
- Honey or maple syrup, to taste (optional)

## Instructions:

- Place a saucepan on medium heat and pour water or milk into it. Let it come to a boil.
- Once the liquid has come to a boil, add the rolled oats to the saucepan and reduce the heat to low.
- Stir the mixture occasionally and let it simmer for about 5 minutes until the oats cook and the mixture thickens to your desired consistency.
- While the oatmeal is cooking, prepare your desired

toppings.

- Slice the banana and chop the nuts and dried fruit.
- Once the oatmeal is cooked, divide it evenly between two bowls.
- Add chopped nuts, dried fruit, and sliced banana to each bowl of oatmeal.
- Drizzle honey or maple syrup over the oatmeal to sweeten, if desired.
- Serve the oatmeal with fruit and nuts immediately while it's warm.

## Variations:

- **Berries A Plenty:** For added sweetness and antioxidants, mix a small amount of frozen or fresh berries (strawberries, blueberries, or raspberries) into the oatmeal.
- **Coconut Crunch:** Sprinkle shredded coconut over the oatmeal for a tropical flavor and additional texture.
- **Chocolate Indulgence:** Stir in a tablespoon of cocoa powder or add chocolate chips to the oatmeal for a rich and decadent treat.
- **Pumpkin Spice:** Mix in pumpkin puree and a sprinkle

of pumpkin pie spice for a cozy fall-inspired oatmeal.

- **Nut Butter Bliss:** To add extra creaminess and protein to your oatmeal, swirl in a spoonful of your preferred nut butter (like peanut butter or almond butter).

(Note: Nutritional values may vary depending on specific ingredients and portion sizes.)

# Crunchy Cornflake Bacon

- **Prep Time:** 5 minutes
- **Cook Time:** 15 minutes
- **Total Time:** 20 minutes
- **Servings:** 2
- Calories: Approximately 200

## Ingredients:

- 6 slices of bacon
- 1 cup cornflakes, crushed
- 1/4 teaspoon black pepper
- 1/4 teaspoon garlic powder
- Maple syrup or honey for drizzling (optional)

## Instructions:

- First, preheat the oven to 375°F (190°C). Once the oven is preheated, line it with parchment paper.
- Next, place the cornflakes in a resealable plastic bag and crush them into small pieces using a rolling pin or your hands.
- Combine the crushed cornflakes, black pepper, and garlic powder in a shallow dish.
- Pat the strips of bacon into the crushed cornflakes, ensuring that each strip is evenly coated. Gently press

the flakes onto the bacon to ensure they adhere well. (Optional: If you prefer, you can also dip the coated bacon strips into a mixture of milk, ketchup, Worcestershire sauce, and pepper. This will add an extra layer of flavor to your bacon. Once coated, proceed with cooking as directed.)

- Once the baking sheet is ready, arrange the coated bacon slices.
- Bake for 12 to 15 minutes until the cornflakes are golden brown and the bacon is crisp.
- After baking, let the bacon cool.
- Optionally, drizzle with maple syrup or honey for sweetness.
- Serve the cornflake-coated crispy bacon hot, and enjoy!

## Variations:

- **Spicy Twist:** Add a pinch of cayenne pepper or paprika to the cornflake mixture for a spicy kick.
- **Tangy Glaze:** In a small bowl, mix 2 tablespoons of ketchup and 1 tablespoon of Worcestershire sauce. Use this mixture as a glaze for the bacon before coating it with the cornflake mixture. Bake as directed. The tangy

ketchup and savory Worcestershire sauce will add a delicious twist to your crispy bacon.

- **Savory Umami:** Add 1 tablespoon of Worcestershire sauce, black pepper, and garlic powder to the cornflake mixture. This will impart a rich umami flavor to the bacon, enhancing its savory profile. Bake as directed for a delicious and satisfying snack or breakfast treat.
- **Smoky Flavor:** Sprinkle smoked paprika or chipotle powder over the bacon before coating it with cornflakes for a smoky flavor.
- **Herb Infusion:** Mix chopped fresh herbs like thyme or rosemary into the cornflake coating for added aroma and flavor.
- **Cheesy Bacon:** Sprinkle-grated Parmesan or cheddar cheese over the bacon before baking for a cheesy twist.

# Orange French Toast Delight

- **Prep Time:** 10 minutes
- **Cook Time:** 10 minutes
- **Total Time:** 20 minutes
- **Servings:** 2
- **Calories:** 310

## Ingredients:

- 4 slices of bread (such as brioche or white sandwich bread)
- 2 large eggs
- 1/4 cup whipped cream cheese (dairy or plant-based)
- 2 tablespoons of orange marmalade
- Butter or oil for cooking

## Instructions:

- Whisk eggs and whipped cream cheese in a shallow dish until smooth.
- Next, spread 1 tablespoon of orange marmalade on 2 slices of bread.
- Top with the last 2 bread slices to make sandwiches.
- Now, dip each sandwich into the egg mixture, ensuring that every part of the bread is coated.
- Next, Lightly grease or butter a nonstick skillet or griddle and place it over medium heat. Place the dipped

- sandwiches on the heated skillet and fry for 3–4 minutes per side until golden brown and crispy.
- Once the French toast sandwiches are cooked, remove them from the skillet and slice them diagonally.
- Add powdered sugar, orange marmalade, or whipped cream, and serve warm. Enjoy!

## Variations:

- **Nutty Crunch:** Sprinkle chopped nuts (such as almonds, pecans, or walnuts) over the marmalade before assembling the sandwiches for added texture.
- **Banana Bliss:** Add thinly sliced bananas between the marmalade layers for a fruity twist.
- **Coconut Delight:** Spread a thin layer of coconut cream or shredded coconut over the marmalade for a tropical flavor.
- **Cinnamon Spice:** Add a pinch of cinnamon to the egg mixture for warmth and aroma.
- **Berry Burst:** Serve the French toast sandwiches with a side of mixed berries or a drizzle of berry compote for a refreshing accompaniment.

# Mushroom Spinach Egg Pie

- **Prep Time:** 10 minutes
- **Cook Time:** 20 minutes
- **Total Time:** 30 minutes
- **Servings:** 2
- **Calories**: Approximately 250

## Ingredients:

- 4 large eggs
- 1 cup spinach leaves, chopped
- 1/2 cup mushrooms, sliced
- 1/4 cup shredded cheese (such as cheddar or mozzarella)
- 2 tablespoons of olive oil
  - Salt and pepper to taste

## Instructions:

- Preheat the oven to 350°F (175°C).
- Once the oven is heated, place an oven-safe skillet on the stove and heat 1 tablespoon of olive oil over medium heat. Add sliced mushrooms to the skillet and cook for 3–4 minutes until softened.
- To continue, add the chopped spinach to the skillet alongside the mushrooms. Stirring occasionally, cook for two to three minutes until the spinach wilts. Place cooked veggies on a dish.

- In a mixing bowl, beat the eggs thoroughly and season them with salt and pepper according to your preference.
- Same skillet: Heat the remaining olive oil over medium heat. Once the oil is heated, pour the beaten eggs into the skillet and allow them to cook undisturbed until the edges set for about 2–3 minutes.
- Once the edges of the eggs are set, add the sautéed spinach and mushrooms evenly over the eggs. Then, evenly distribute the shredded cheese on top of the veggies.
- Place the skillet in the oven for 10–12 minutes to allow the eggs to set and the cheese to melt. Once baked, let the frittata cool for a few minutes before cutting it into wedges. Serve it hot and enjoy!

## Variations:

- **Herb Infusion:** To flavor the egg mixture, add chopped fresh herbs like parsley, basil, or dill.
- **Meaty Option:** Cook bacon, ham, or sausage to add more flavor and protein to the frittata.
- **Cheese Lover's Delight:** To alter the taste of your frittata, try experimenting with different kinds of

cheese, like feta, Swiss, or goat cheese.

- **Veg Medley:** For a vibrant and wholesome frittata, stir in additional veggies like bell peppers, onions, or cherry tomatoes.
- **Spice it up:** Add hot sauce or red pepper flakes for a spicy frittata.

(Note: Nutritional values are approximate and may vary depending on specific ingredients and portion sizes.)

# Blueberry Bliss Yogurt Bowl

- **Prep Time:** 5 minutes
- **Servings:** 2
- **Calories**: 180

## Ingredients:

- 1 cup Greek yogurt
- 1/2 cup fresh blueberries
- 2 tablespoons of honey

## Instructions:

- Divide the Greek yogurt evenly between two serving bowls.
- Wash the fresh blueberries and pat them dry with a paper towel.
- Sprinkle the blueberries over the yogurt in each bowl.
- Drizzle 1 tablespoon of honey over each yogurt bowl.
- Serve immediately as a nutritious and delicious breakfast or snack.

## Variations:

- **Nutty Crunch:** Sprinkle chopped nuts (such as almonds, walnuts, or pecans) over the yogurt for added texture and protein.

- **Tropical Twist:** Add diced pineapple or mango chunks to the yogurt for a tropical flavor.
- **Granola Goodness:** Top the yogurt with a handful of granola for a satisfying crunch.
- **Cinnamon Spice:** Stir a pinch of ground cinnamon into the yogurt before adding the blueberries for a warm and aromatic flavor.
- **Coconut Delight:** For a hint of tropical sweetness, garnish the yogurt with shredded coconut or a drizzle of coconut milk.

(Note: Nutritional values are approximate and may vary depending on specific ingredients and serving sizes.)

# Berry Burst Chia Pudding

- **Prep Time:** 5 minutes
- **Total Time:** 4 hours, 5 minutes (including chilling time)
- **Servings**: 2
- **Calories:** 180

## Ingredients:

- 1/4 cup chia seeds
- 1 cup almond milk (or any milk of your choice)
- 1 tablespoon maple syrup (or honey)
- 1/2 teaspoon vanilla extract
- 1/2 cup fresh blueberries

## Instructions:

- Combine the chia seeds, creamy almond milk, sweet maple syrup (or honey), and fragrant vanilla extract in a mixing bowl. Stir the mixture to spread the chia seeds evenly.
- Refrigerate the bowl for four hours or overnight to thicken the chia seeds.
- Once the pudding has been set, divide it into two serving glasses or bowls, and top each serving with a generous amount of fresh blueberries.
- Serve the chilled blueberry chia seed pudding as a

wholesome breakfast to start your day or as a delectable dessert to end your meal on a high note.

## Variations:

- **Mixed Berry Medley:** Use a combination of different berries, such as strawberries, raspberries, and blackberries, for a colorful twist.
- **Coconut Delight:** Half almond milk replaces coconut milk for creaminess.
- **Chocolate Indulgence:** For a chocolaty treat, stir in one tablespoon of cocoa powder to the pudding mixture.
- **Nutty Crunch:** Sprinkle chopped nuts (such as almonds, walnuts, or pecans) over the top for added crunch and protein.
- **Citrus Zest:** Add a teaspoon of lemon or orange zest to the pudding for a refreshing citrus flavor.

(Note: Nutritional values are approximate and may vary depending on specific ingredients and portion sizes.)

# Banana Nut Oatmeal Delight

- **Prep Time**: 5 minutes
- **Cook Time:** 5 minutes
- **Total Time:** 10 minutes
- **Servings:** 2
- **Calories:** Approximately 350

## Ingredients:

- 1 cup rolled oats
- 2 cups milk (dairy or plant-based)
- 2 ripe bananas, mashed
- 2 tablespoons of peanut butter
- 2 tablespoons of honey or maple syrup
- Optional toppings: sliced bananas, chopped nuts, chocolate chips, shredded coconut

## Instructions:

- In a saucepan, heat the milk over medium heat until it begins to boil gently. While stirring, add the rolled oats. Lower the heat to a low simmer and cook, stirring occasionally, until the mixture thickens and the oats are soft, about 5 minutes.
- While cooking oatmeal, use a fork to mash ripe bananas in a small bowl until smooth.
- Once the oatmeal is fully cooked, stir in the mashed

bananas and peanut butter and evenly combined. Cook for another 1-2 minutes to mix.

- To add sweetness, drizzle honey or maple syrup over the oatmeal and stir it until it is thoroughly mixed in.
- To serve, divide the Silly Monkey Oatmeal into bowls and add your favorite toppings, such as sliced bananas, chopped nuts, chocolate chips, or shredded coconut.
- Enjoy your oatmeal bowl immediately!

## Variations:

- **Chocolate Monkey:** Mix cocoa powder or chocolate chips into the oatmeal for a chocolaty twist.
- **Nutty Monkey:** Sprinkle chopped nuts (such as peanuts, almonds, or walnuts) over the oatmeal for extra crunch and protein.
- **Berries and Cream:** For a fruity variation, top the oatmeal with fresh berries (such as strawberries or raspberries) and a dollop of Greek yogurt.
- **Cinnamon Spice:** Add a sprinkle of ground cinnamon to the oatmeal for a warm and cozy flavor.
- **Coconut Banana Bliss:** Mix shredded coconut into the oatmeal and top with toasted coconut flakes for a tropical twist.

(Note: Nutritional values are approximate and may vary depending on specific ingredients and portion sizes.)

# Coconut Milk Nutty Oats

- **Prep Time:** 5 minutes
- **Cook Time:** 10 minutes
- **Total Time:** 15 minutes
- **Servings:** 2
- **Calories**: 350

## Ingredients:

- 1 cup rolled oats
- 1 1/2 cups coconut milk
- 2 tablespoons of honey or maple syrup
- 1/4 cup sliced almonds
- Pinch of salt
- Optional toppings: additional sliced almonds, shredded coconut, fresh berries, or banana slices.

## Instructions:

- In a saucepan, mix rolled oats, creamy coconut milk, and a sweetener like honey or maple syrup. Sprinkle a pinch of salt to enhance the flavor, and bring the mixture to a gentle boil over medium heat.
- Lower the heat and simmer for 5-7 minutes, stirring occasionally, until the oats are cooked and the mixture thickens to your liking.
- While your oatmeal is cooking, you can prepare the

almonds. Add sliced almonds to a small skillet over medium heat. Toast until golden brown and fragrant, stirring frequently, for 3–5 minutes. Turn off the skillet and set the almonds aside.

- Once your oatmeal is ready, divide it between two bowls and top each serving with the toasted almonds.
- Add shredded coconut, fresh berries, or banana slices for extra flavor and nutrition.
- Serve the coconut milk oatmeal with almonds immediately while it's still warm, and enjoy a healthy and satisfying breakfast.

## Variations:

- **Fruity Twist:** Stir in some chopped dried fruit, such as apricots, dates, or raisins, for added sweetness and flavor.
- **Nutty Crunch:** Replace the sliced almonds with chopped walnuts, pecans, or hazelnuts for a different nutty flavor.
- **Spiced Oatmeal:** Add cinnamon or nutmeg to the oatmeal while cooking for a warm and comforting flavor.
- **Creamy Coconut:** Drizzle extra coconut milk over the oatmeal before serving for a creamier texture and extra coconut flavor.

# Bacon Cheddar Breakfast Cups

- **Prep Time:** 15 minutes
- **Cook Time:** 25 minutes
- **Total Time:** 40 minutes
- **Servings:** 2
- **Calories**: 290

## Ingredients:

- 3 slices of bacon, cooked and crumbled
- 1/2 cup shredded cheddar cheese
- 2 large eggs
- 2 tablespoons of milk
- Salt and pepper, to taste
- Cooking spray or melted butter for greasing

## Instructions:

- First, preheat your oven to 375°F (190°C) and grease two cups in a muffin tin with cooking spray or melted butter to prevent sticking.
- If you do, have cooked bacon. Cook until crispy bacon is golden brown. Once done, crumble or chop it. Fry or bake—your choice!
- Next, use a grater to shred cheddar cheese finely.
- Whisk eggs in a bowl until frothy. Then, pour in the milk and whisk again until everything is combined. Add

a pinch of salt and pepper to taste and whisk once again until the mixture is consistent and smooth.

- Divide the crumbled bacon and shredded cheddar cheese evenly between the two greased muffin tin cups, filling each halfway. Then, pour the egg mixture over the bacon and cheese in each muffin cup, filling them nearly to the top but only partially.

- Now, Bake the muffin tin quiche cups for 20–25 minutes until set and lightly golden. Check quiche doneness with a toothpick. If clean, quiche cups are done.

- Carefully remove the quiche cups from the muffin tin a few minutes later. You can use a knife or a spoon to help loosen them from the tin. Serve them warm and enjoy!

## Variations:

- **Veggie Lovers:** Add diced vegetables, such as bell peppers, spinach, or tomatoes, to the quiche cups for flavor and nutrition.

- **Ham and Cheese:** Substitute cooked ham or Canadian bacon for the bacon and use Swiss cheese instead of cheddar for a classic combination.

- **Mushroom and Spinach:** Sauté sliced mushrooms and spinach until softened, then add them to the quiche cups along with the cheese before pouring in the egg mixture.
- **Sausage and Pepper Jack:** Replace the bacon with cooked crumbled sausage and use pepper jack cheese for a spicy kick.
- **Caprese Style:** Add diced tomatoes, fresh basil, and mozzarella cheese to the quiche cups for a delightful twist.

(Note: Nutritional values are approximate and may vary depending on specific ingredients and portion sizes.)

# Berrylicious Muesli Trio

- **Prep Time:** 5 minutes
- **Chill Time:** Overnight
- **Total Time:** 8 hours, 5 minutes
- **Servings:** 2
- **Calories:** 250

## Ingredients:

- 1 cup muesli
- 1 cup mixed berries (such as strawberries, blueberries, or raspberries)
- 1 cup milk (dairy or plant-based)

## Instructions:

- Firstly, wash berries thoroughly under running water and dry them with a paper towel. For strawberries, remove the hull and slice them into smaller pieces.
- Next, Add the mixed berries and muesli to a covered bowl or container. Mix the ingredients well to ensure the berries are evenly distributed throughout the muesli.
- Then, pour the milk over the muesli mixture and mix well. Stir the mixture thoroughly so that the muesli absorbs the milk.
- Cover the bowl or container with a lid and refrigerate the muesli mixture overnight or for at least 8 hours.

- Stir the muesli before serving.
- **Optional:** sprinkle honey or maple syrup for sweetness.
- Finally, divide the overnight berry muesli into bowls and serve chilled. Add toppings, such as nuts, seeds, or a dollop of yogurt.

## Variations:

- **Nutty Crunch:** Before serving, sprinkle chopped almonds, walnuts, or pecans over muesli for texture and taste.
- **Coconut Delight:** Stir in a tablespoon of shredded coconut into the muesli mixture before refrigerating for a tropical twist.
- **Chocolate Indulgence:** Add a tablespoon of cocoa powder or chocolate chips to the muesli mixture for a decadent chocolatey flavor.
- **Banana Bliss:** Slice a ripe banana and layer it with the muesli before refrigerating overnight. Bananas add natural sweetness and creaminess.
- **Spiced Infusion:** Mix in a pinch of cinnamon or nutmeg to the muesli mixture for warm, comforting flavors reminiscent of oatmeal cookies.

# Raspberries and Oats Delight

- **Prep Time:** 5 minutes
- **Servings:** 2
- **Calories**: Approximately 250

## Ingredients:

- 1 cup muesli
- 1 cup of raspberries
- 1 cup milk (dairy or plant-based)

## Instructions:

- Wash the fresh raspberries under cold running water and use a paper towel to pat them dry.
- Next, take a mixing bowl, add muesli and raspberries to the bowl, and mix them well.
- Pour the milk over the muesli and raspberries.
- Stir everything together until the muesli is evenly coated with milk and the raspberries are distributed throughout.
- Divide the muesli with raspberries into bowls and serve immediately.
- Enjoy your refreshing and nutritious muesli with raspberries!

# Variations:

- **Nutty Crunch:** Add a handful of chopped nuts, such as almonds, walnuts, or pecans, for extra texture and flavor.
- **Coconut Bliss:** Sprinkle shredded coconut over the muesli for a tropical twist.
- **Banana Boost:** Slice a ripe banana and add it to the muesli for sweetness and creaminess.
- **Berry Medley:** Mix different berries, such as blackberries, blueberries, and strawberries, to make a vibrant and tasty mixture.
- **Yogurt Swirl:** For extra creaminess and protein, top the muesli with a dollop of Greek yogurt and serve.

(Note: Nutritional values are approximate and may vary depending on specific ingredients and portion sizes.)

# Mushroom Spinach Egg Scramble

- **Prep Time:** 5 minutes
- **Cook Time:** 5 minutes
- **Total Time:** 10 minutes
- **Servings:** 2
- **Calories**: approximately 220

## Ingredients:

- 4 large eggs
- 1 cup fresh spinach, chopped
- 1 cup mushrooms, sliced
- 2 tablespoons of butter or olive oil
- Salt and pepper to taste
- Optional: shredded cheese for topping

## Instructions:

- First, take a bunch of fresh spinach leaves and mushrooms and rinse them thoroughly in water.

- Finely chop spinach and finely slice mushrooms.

- Pour a little butter or olive oil into a skillet over medium heat. After the butter or oil melts, add the sliced mushrooms and cook for 2–3 minutes, stirring occasionally.

- Next, add the chopped spinach and cook until it wilts, stirring through. This takes about 1–2 minutes.

- Crack and whisk the eggs in a separate bowl until well combined—season with salt and pepper to taste.
- Add beaten eggs to skillet. Scratching the skillet bottom, stir the mixture until the eggs are done. This should take 2–3 minutes.
- Once the scrambled eggs are cooked, remove the skillet from the heat and divide them evenly between two plates. While the eggs are hot, sprinkle some shredded cheese on them if desired.
- Serve immediately and enjoy!

## Variations:

- **Cheesy Scrambled Eggs:** To add more creaminess and flavor, stir in your preferred cheese, feta, or cheddar.
- **Herb-infused Scrambled Eggs:** Add chopped fresh herbs like parsley, chives, or basil to the beaten eggs before cooking for added freshness.
- **Spicy Scrambled Eggs:** Mix in some diced jalapeños or red pepper flakes for a kick of heat.
- **Protein Boost:** Add cooked bacon, ham, or sausage to the scrambled eggs for additional protein and flavor.
- **Vegetarian Option:** Add chopped jalapeños or red pepper flakes for a spicy kick.

# Egg Chorizo Breakfast Wraps

- **Prep Time:** 10 minutes
- **Cook Time:** 10 minutes
- **Total Time:** 20 minutes
- **Servings:** 2
- **Calories**: Approximately 450

## Ingredients:

- 4 large eggs
- 4 oz. chorizo sausage, sliced
- 1/2 cup shredded cheddar cheese
- 4 small flour tortillas
- Salt and pepper to taste
- Salsa and sour cream for serving (optional)

## Instructions:

- Cook the chorizo slices in a pan for 5-7 minutes, or until they are crispy and browned. Set aside.
- Pour the cracked eggs into the same pan and cook through. Season with salt and pepper.
- Heat tortillas until soft and warm.
- Divide cooked chorizo and eggs among tortillas. Add shredded cheese.
- Roll tortillas tightly to form wraps.
- Enjoy immediately with salsa and sour cream on the

side.

## Variations:

- **Vegetarian Option:** Use vegetarian chorizo or sautéed veggies instead of chorizo.
- **Spicy Kick:** Add chopped jalapeños or chili powder for a spicy kick.
- **Avocado Addition:** Include avocado slices or guacamole for creaminess.
- **Breakfast Burrito:** Add cooked potatoes or black beans for a heartier meal.

# Quick Egg Cheese Delight

- **Prep Time:** 5 minutes
- **Cook Time:** 10 minutes
- **Total Time:** 15 minutes
- **Servings:** 2
- **Calories**: Approximately 250

## Ingredients:

- 4 eggs
- 1/4 cup of milk
- 1/2 cup shredded cheese (cheddar, mozzarella, or your choice)
- Salt and pepper to taste
- Chopped fresh herbs (optional, for garnish)

## Instructions:

- Preheat the oven to 350°F (175°C) and lightly grease two ramekins or oven-safe dishes.
- In a bowl, mix eggs and milk until smooth and Season with salt and pepper to taste.
- Next, stir in some shredded cheese to add flavor and creaminess.
- Pour the egg and cheese mixture evenly into the prepared ramekins, leaving some room at the top.
- Bake the ramekins for 10 minutes to set the eggs and melt the cheese.

- After cooking, carefully take the ramekins out of the oven, and if you'd like, top with finely chopped fresh herbs.
- Enjoy your tasty and filling breakfast while it's hot!

## Variations:

- **Veggie Delight:** Add diced bell peppers, onions, tomatoes, or spinach to the egg mixture for flavor and nutrition.
- **Meaty Option:** Incorporate cooked bacon, ham, sausage, or turkey sausage crumbles into the egg mixture for a heartier dish.
- **Spice it up:** Sprinkle red pepper flakes or add a dash of hot sauce to the egg mixture for a kick of heat.
- **Herb Infusion:** Mix chopped fresh herbs such as parsley, chives, basil, or dill into the egg mixture for extra flavor.
- **Cheese Lovers' Dream:** Experiment with different types of cheese, such as Swiss, feta, or pepperjack, to customize the flavor profile.

(Note: Nutritional values are approximate and may vary depending on specific ingredients and portion sizes.)

# Ham and Cheese Breakfast Bun

- **Prep Time:** 5 minutes
- **Cook Time:** 5 minutes
- **Total Time:** 10 minutes
- **Servings:** 2
- **Calories**: Approximately 350

## Ingredients:

- 4 slices of bread (whole grain or your choice)
- 4 slices of ham
- 2 slices of cheese (cheddar, Swiss, or your favorite)
- 2 large eggs
- Butter or cooking spray for greasing
- Salt and pepper to taste

## Instructions:

- Heat a non-stick skillet over medium heat.
- Grease the skillet with butter or cooking spray.
- Pour the eggs into the skillet and cook until set. Cook until the desired doneness. If you like, flip the eggs to cook both sides evenly. Season the eggs with salt and pepper.
- Toast bread until golden.
- On toasted bread, place slices of ham.
- Next, place the cooked eggs over the ham.

- Finally, add a slice of cheese on top of the eggs.
- Place another ham slice on top of the cheese.
- To finish the sandwich, top with the second toasted piece of bread. Repeat these steps to remaining sandwich.
- Serve warm ham and cheese breakfast sandwiches with melted cheese immediately.

## Variations:

- **Veggie Delight:** Add sautéed vegetables like spinach, mushrooms, or bell peppers to the sandwich for extra flavor and nutrients.
- **Spicy Kick:** Spread a layer of spicy mustard or Sriracha mayo on the bread for a spicy twist.
- **Double Cheese:** For a cheesier sandwich, add an extra slice of cheese or choose a cheese with a more robust flavor, like pepper jack
- **Turkey Substitution:** Replace the ham with sliced turkey for a different flavor profile.
- **Croissant Upgrade:** Swap the bread for a croissant for a flakier, more indulgent breakfast sandwich.

# Mascarpone Berry Toast Treat

- **Prep Time:** 5 minutes
- **Cook Time:** N/A
- **Total Time:** 5 minutes
- **Servings:** 2
- **Calories**: Approximately 300

## Ingredients:

- 4 slices of bread (such as whole grain or sourdough), toasted
- 1/2 cup mascarpone cheese
- 1 cup mixed berries (such as strawberries, blueberries, or raspberries)
- Honey or maple syrup, for drizzling
- Fresh mint leaves, for garnish (optional)

## Instructions:

- Toast the bread until golden brown. Use any bread, but a crusty, rustic bread is best for this recipe.
- Spread mascarpone cheese generously on each slice of toasted bread.
- Next, add the mixed berries to the toast. Use strawberries, blueberries, raspberries, or blackberries.
- Add honey or maple syrup to the berries to sweeten the toast.
- Optional garnish: Use fresh mint leaves to decorate the

berries.
- Finally, it serves as a delicious breakfast or snack.

## Variations:

- **Chocolate Indulgence:** For a decadent treat, sprinkle dark chocolate shavings or cocoa nibs over the mascarpone and berries.
- **Nutty Crunch:** Sprinkle chopped nuts such as almonds, walnuts, or pecans over the mascarpone and berries for added texture.
- **Cinnamon Twist:** Sprinkle ground cinnamon over the mascarpone layer before adding the berries for a warm and aromatic flavor.
- **Citrus Zest:** Grate lemon or orange zest on toast to enhance lemon flavor.
- **Coconut Bliss:** Sprinkle shredded coconut over the mascarpone and berries for a tropical flavor and additional texture.

(Note: Nutritional values are approximate and may vary depending on specific ingredients and portion sizes.)

# Almond Butter Grape Delight

- **Prep Time:** 5 minutes
- **Cook Time:** 15 minutes
- **Total Time:** 20 minutes
- **Servings:** 2
- **Calories**: Approximately 250

## Ingredients:

- 4 slices of whole-grain bread
- 2 tablespoons of almond butter
- 1 cup red grapes, seedless
- 1 tablespoon of honey
- A pinch of cinnamon (optional)
- Fresh mint leaves for garnish (optional)

## Instructions:

- Preheat your oven to 375°F (190°C).
- Next, wash the grapes thoroughly to remove any dirt or debris. Use a paper towel to gently pat the grapes dry after washing. This will help to remove any excess water that might prevent the grapes from roasting correctly.
- Once the grapes are dry, arrange them on a baking sheet. Make sure to use a baking sheet lined with parchment paper to prevent the grapes from sticking to the sheet. Spread the grapes evenly on the baking sheet,

ensuring enough space between each grape for even cooking. Once the grapes are arranged, bake the baking sheet for 15-20 minutes until they soften and release their juices. Allow them to cool slightly.

- Toast the bread in a toaster or skillet over medium heat until golden brown.
- After toasting, spread almond butter on a toasted bread slice.
- Arrange the roasted grapes evenly over the almond butter layer on each toast.
- Drizzle honey over the top of the roasted grapes. If desired, add a pinch of cinnamon.
- Decorate toast with mint leaves for color and freshness.
- Serve it as a healthy breakfast or snack.

## Variations:

- **Creamy Cheese:** Add a smear of cream or ricotta cheese under the almond butter for extra creaminess.
- **Berry Bonanza:** Mix in roasted or fresh berries, such as strawberries, blueberries, or raspberries, and the grapes for various flavors.
- **Savory Twist:** Instead of honey, drizzle balsamic glaze

over the toasts for a sweet and tangy contrast.

- **Chocolate Indulgence:** Add a sprinkle of dark chocolate shavings or cocoa nibs over the almond butter and roasted grapes for a decadent treat.

(Note: Nutritional values are approximate and may vary depending on specific ingredients and portion sizes.)

# Sunny-Side Up Open-Face Breakfast

- **Prep Time:** 5 minutes
- **Cook Time:** 10 minutes
- **Total Time:** 15 minutes
- **Servings:** 2
- **Calories**: Approximately 300

## Ingredients:

- 2 slices of whole-grain bread
- 2 large eggs
- 1 ripe avocado
- 1 small tomato, sliced
- Salt and pepper to taste
- Optional toppings: shredded cheese, cooked bacon or ham, arugula, hot sauce

## Instructions:

- Slice one avocado in half, remove the pit, and spoon the flesh into a dish.
- Mash the avocado with a fork and season with salt and pepper to taste. Set aside.
- Over medium heat, crack eggs into a non-stick skillet and cook for 2–3 minutes until whites are cooked but yolks are runny. Season with salt and pepper.
- Toast bread until golden.
- Once toasted, generously layer each slice with mashed

avocado. Add a cooked egg and some tomato slices on top.
- Add optional toppings such as sliced cheese, cooked bacon or ham, arugula, or hot sauce.
- Finally, serve the open-faced egg sandwiches with salt and pepper if desired.

## Variations:

- **Cheesy Delight:** Sprinkle shredded cheese over the avocado before adding the egg for a melty, cheesy finish.
- **Meaty Twist:** Add cooked bacon, ham, or sausage patties to the avocado for a heartier sandwich.
- **Green Goddess:** Add a handful of fresh spinach or arugula on top of the avocado for extra greens and a burst of freshness.
- **Spicy Kick:** Drizzle hot sauce or sprinkle red pepper flakes over the eggs for a spicy kick.
- **Caprese Style:** Replace the sliced tomato with fresh basil leaves and shredded mozzarella cheese, and top with a drizzle of balsamic glaze.

(Note: Nutritional values are approximate and may vary depending on specific ingredients and portion sizes.)

# Lentil Goat Cheese Morning Melt

- **Prep Time:** 10 minutes
- **Cook Time:** 20 minutes
- **Total Time:** 30 minutes
- **Servings:** 2
- **Calories**: Approximately 300

## Ingredients:

- 4 slices of bread (such as whole wheat or sourdough)
- 1 cup cooked lentils
- 2 ounces of goat cheese
- 1 tablespoon of olive oil
- 1 garlic clove, minced
- Salt and pepper to taste
- Fresh parsley or basil for garnish (optional)

## Instructions:

- If you're using canned lentils, drain and rinse them. If you're using dry lentils, cook them according to the package instructions until tender. Set aside.
- Toast the slices of bread until golden brown and crispy.
- Heat olive oil in a skillet on medium. Cook minced garlic for 1-2 minutes until fragrant. Add lentils in the pan and cook lentils for 3–4 minutes, stirring periodically, until warm.
- Apply the lentil mixture to each toasted bread slice.

- Crumble the goat cheese over the lentil mixture on each toast.
- Sprinkle with fresh parsley or basil for garnish, if desired.
- Serve it open-faced as a sandwich or snack.

## Variations:

- **Herb Infusion:** Mix chopped fresh herbs (such as parsley, thyme, or rosemary) into the lentil mixture for added flavor.
- **Roasted Veggie Boost:** Before adding the goat cheese, top the lentil mixture with roasted vegetables (such as cherry tomatoes, bell peppers, or zucchini).
- **Spicy Kick:** Add red pepper flakes or hot sauce for a spicy kick.
- **Nutty Crunch:** For a crunchy texture, sprinkle chopped nuts like walnuts or almonds over goat cheese.
- **Balsamic Glaze:** Drizzle with balsamic glaze before serving for a tart and sweet finish.

(Note: Nutritional values are approximate and may vary depending on specific ingredients and portion sizes.)

# Simple Cereal Snack Bars

- **Prep Time:** 10 minutes
- **Cook Time:** 5 minutes (melting ingredients)
- **Total Time:** 1-2 hours (chilling time)
- **Servings:** Makes about 12 bars
- **Calories:** Approximately 200

## Ingredients:

- 2 cups of crispy rice cereal
- 1 cup old-fashioned oats
- 1/2 cup honey or maple syrup
- 1/2 cup peanut butter or almond butter
- 1/2 cup mini chocolate chips (optional)
- 1 teaspoon vanilla extract (optional)

## Instructions:

- Mix peanut butter or almond butter with honey or maple syrup in a microwave-safe bowl or saucepan. Melt and smooth the mixture in the microwave or stovetop, stirring occasionally.

- Combine the old-fashioned oats and crispy rice cereal in a large mixing bowl.

- Over the cereal and oat mixture, drizzle the melted honey or maple syrup mixture. Use a spatula to combine all of it.

- Add the vanilla extract for extra flavor and the mini chocolate chips for sweetness, if desired.
- Cover a baking dish or pan with parchment paper or aluminum foil, leaving an overhang for easy removal. Transfer the cereal mixture to the prepared dish and press it down firmly and evenly using the back of a spoon or spatula.
- Refrigerate the cereal bars for 1-2 hours until firm.
- Remove the cereal bars and cut the bars into servings with a sharp knife.
- Refrigerate no-bake cereal bars for a week in an airtight container. Try them anytime as a quick snack!

## Variations:

- **Nutty Crunch:** Add chopped nuts, such as almonds, peanuts, or cashews, to the cereal mixture for extra texture and protein.
- **Fruity Twist:** Mix dried fruits like raisins, cranberries, or chopped apricots into the cereal mixture for a natural sweetness.
- **Coconut Delight:** Stir in shredded coconut flakes to the cereal mixture for a tropical flavor and aroma.

- **Protein Boost:** Incorporate protein powder into the honey or maple syrup mixture for an added protein kick.
- **Trail Mix Bars:** Customize the cereal bars by adding nuts, seeds, dried fruits, and chocolate chips for a homemade trail mix bar experience.

(Note: Nutritional values may vary depending on specific ingredients and portion sizes.)

## Sweet Bacon Grits Puff

- **Prep Time:** 10 minutes
- **Cook Time:** 30 minutes
- **Total Time:** 40 minutes
- **Servings:** 2
- **Calories:** Approximately 250

## Ingredients:

- 1/2 cup quick-cooking grits
- 2 slices of bacon, chopped
- 1 tablespoon of maple syrup
- 1/4 cup shredded cheddar cheese
- 1 large egg
- Salt and pepper to taste

## Instructions:

- Preheat the oven to 375°F (190°C). Spray or butter two ramekins or small baking dishes with cooking spray.
- Next, bring one cup of water to a boil in a saucepan. Add 1/2 cup quick-cooking grits, reduce the heat to low, and simmer for 5-7 minutes, stirring occasionally until thickening.
- Fry the chopped bacon in a skillet until crispy. Remove it from the pan and drain the grease.
- After cooking the grits, remove them from the heat. Stir

in the cooked bacon, 1 tablespoon maple syrup, and 1/4 cup shredded cheddar cheese until well combined.

- Crack 1 large egg into the grits mixture and Season with salt and pepper to taste stir until evenly mix.
- Add the grit mixture to the ramekins, filling them 3/4 of the way.
- Bake until in a preheated oven for 45-55 minutes or golden brown and puffy.
- Serve the grit puffs after they cool from the oven.

## Variation:

- **Herb Infusion:** Add chopped fresh herbs like thyme or chives to the grits mixture for a herby twist.
- **Sausage Swap:** Instead of bacon, use cooked breakfast sausage crumbles for a different flavor profile.
- **Veggie Boost:** Add sautéed vegetables like onions, bell peppers, or spinach to the grits mixture for added texture and nutrients.
- **Smoky Flavor:** For a smoky twist, incorporate a dash of smoked paprika or liquid smoke into the grits mixture.

(Note: Nutritional values are approximate and may vary depending on specific ingredients and portion sizes.)

# Blueberry Muffin French Delight

- **Prep Time:** 10 minutes
- **Cook Time:** 10 minutes
- **Total Time:** 20 minutes
- **Servings:** 2
- **Calories:** Approximately 300

## Ingredients:

- 4 slices of blueberry muffins (store-bought or homemade)
- 2 large eggs
- 1/4 cup of milk
- 1/2 teaspoon vanilla extract
- Butter or cooking spray for greasing
- Maple syrup and fresh blueberries for serving (optional)

## Instructions:

- Grease a skillet or griddle with butter or cooking spray and pre heat over medium heat.
- In a shallow bowl, whisk two large eggs, 1/4 cup of milk, and one teaspoon of vanilla extract until they are well combined.
- Take your blueberry muffins and slice them into 1-inch-thick pieces. Dip each slice in the egg mixture to coat both sides.
- Next, toast the coated blueberry muffin slices for two to

three minutes per side until cooked through and golden brown.
- Muffin slice thickness affects cooking time.
- After toasting, take the French toast from the griddle or skillet and place it on serving plates.
- Finally, warmly serve the blueberry muffin French toast with maple syrup and fresh blueberries as toppings, if desired.

## Variations:

- **Lemon Zest:** Add some lemon zest to the egg mixture for a hint of citrus flavor.
- **Cinnamon Sugar:** Sprinkle cinnamon sugar over the French toast before serving for extra sweetness and flavor.
- **Cream Cheese Drizzle:** Warm some cream cheese in the microwave and drizzle it over the French toast for a creamy and indulgent topping.

(Note: Nutritional values may vary depending on specific ingredients and portion sizes.)

# Southwest Breakfast Burrito Bowl

- **Prep Time:** 5 minutes
- **Cook Time:** 10 minutes
- **Total Time:** 15 minutes
- **Servings:** 2
- **Calories**: 280

## Ingredients:

- 4 large eggs
- 1/2 cup cooked black beans
- 1/2 cup diced bell peppers (any color)
- Salt and pepper to taste
- 2 large flour tortillas halved and cut into strips

## Instructions:

- In a mixing bowl, whisk the eggs and add the black beans, diced bell peppers, salt, and pepper to taste.
- Over medium heat, preheat a skillet. Add the egg mixture to the skillet and stir occasionally until scrambled.
- Add tortillas, stirring constantly, until eggs are set, about 3 minutes.
- Serve the Southwest tortilla scrambles immediately.

## Variations:

- **Cheesy Twist:** Sprinkle shredded cheese on the scrambled eggs before rolling up the tortillas for an extra-gooey and delicious filling.

- **Avocado Addition:** Add sliced avocado or guacamole to the tortilla wraps for a creamy and nutritious addition.

- **Salsa Sensation:** Top the scrambled egg mixture with salsa before rolling up the tortillas for a burst of flavor.

- **Tex-Mex Twist:** Before rolling up the tortillas, top the scrambled egg mixture with a dollop of sour cream and a sprinkle of chopped fresh cilantro. Serve with salsa for dipping.

- **Veggie Delight:** Add extra vegetables, such as diced tomatoes, onions, and mushrooms, to the scrambled egg mixture for a nutrient-packed meal. Stir in cooked spinach or kale for extra vegetables.

(Note: Nutritional values may vary depending on specific ingredients and portion sizes.)

# Feta Egg Breakfast Burritos

- **Prep Time**: 5 minutes
- **Cook Time:** 5 minutes
- **Total Time:** 10 minutes
- **Servings:** 2
- **Calories:** Approximately 300

## Ingredients:

- 4 large eggs
- 1/4 cup crumbled feta cheese
- 4 whole wheat tortillas (8 inches)
- 1 tablespoon of olive oil
- Salt and pepper to taste

## Instructions:

- In a bowl, beat eggs until well combined. To taste, add more salt and pepper.
- In a nonstick pan, heat olive oil on medium after that. Pour the beaten eggs into the skillet once the oil is hot.
- Stirring occasionally, cook the eggs for a few minutes. Continue stirring until the eggs are scrambled.
- Once the eggs are almost done, evenly sprinkle crumbled feta cheese. Allow the cheese to melt for about a minute or until golden brown.
- Toast the tortillas while the eggs cook. place them in a

microwave for 10–15 seconds or heat them in a separate skillet over low heat until they are soft and pliable.

- Once the eggs and tortillas are ready, divide the scrambled egg mixture evenly between the tortillas. Place the Feta-scrambled egg in the middle of every tortilla. You can add some sliced avocado, chopped tomatoes, or fresh herbs.
- To roll up the tortillas, start by folding the sides of each tortilla to secure the filling. Roll each tortilla tightly from bottom to top to pack the filling.
- Serve the warm, melted scrambled feta egg wraps immediately. Enjoy your delicious and filling breakfast or lunch.

## Variations:

- **Mediterranean Twist:** For a Mediterranean-inspired flavor, add diced tomatoes, chopped spinach, and a sprinkle of oregano to the scrambled eggs.
- **Veggie Lover's Delight:** Saute diced bell peppers, onions, and mushrooms before adding them to the scrambled eggs for extra vegetables and flavor.
- **Protein Boost:** Add cooked and crumbled bacon or

sausage to the scrambled eggs for a heartier and more filling wrap.

(Note: Nutritional values may vary depending on specific ingredients and portion sizes.)

# Spicy Salsa Chorizo Omelette

- **Prep Time:** 5 minutes
- **Cook Time:** 10 minutes
- **Total Time:** 15 minutes
- **Servings:** 2
- **Calories:** Approximately 300

## Ingredients:

- 4 large eggs
- 1/4 cup chorizo, cooked and crumbled
- 1/4 cup of salsa
- 1/4 cup shredded cheese (cheddar or Mexican blend)
- Salt and pepper to taste
- 1 tablespoon of olive oil
- Fresh cilantro for garnish (optional)

## Instructions:

- First, crack the eggs into a bowl and whisk them until they become light and fluffy. Add a pinch of salt and pepper.
- Next, place a non-stick skillet over medium heat with a little olive oil. Once the oil is hot, pour the beaten eggs into the skillet and cook. This typically takes 2-3 minutes, and the edges turn golden brown.
- Evenly distribute the cooked chorizo on one half of the omelet.

- Spoon salsa over the chorizo.
- Add some shredded cheese on top of the salsa for extra flavor.
- Gently fold the remaining omelet over the filling with a spatula. Continue cooking for 1-2 minutes to melt the cheese and finish the omelet.
- Place the omelet on a plate and top with fresh cilantro.

## Variations:

- **Veggie Lovers:** Add diced bell peppers, onions, or tomatoes to the filling for extra flavor and texture.
- **Spicy Twist:** Use spicy salsa or chopped jalapeños for a kick of heat.
- **Mushroom Delight:** Sauté sliced mushrooms and add them to the filling for an earthy flavor.
- **Avocado Addition:** Serve slices of fresh avocado on top of the omelet for creaminess and richness.

(Note: Nutritional values may vary depending on specific ingredients and portion sizes.)

# Breakfast Bacon Pizza

- **Prep Time:** 10 minutes
- **Cook Time:** 15 minutes
- **Total Time:** 25 minutes
- **Servings**: 2
- **Calories**: Approximately 500

## Ingredients:

- 1 pre-made pizza crust (store-bought or homemade)
- 4 slices of bacon, cooked and crumbled
- 4 large eggs
- 1 cup shredded cheddar cheese
- Salt and pepper to taste
- Cooking spray or olive oil for greasing

## Instructions:

- Preheat the oven to 425°F (220°C).
- Now cook the bacon in a skillet until crisp, then break it up.
- Beat the eggs lightly in a bowl and season with salt and pepper.
- Use cooking spray or olive oil to grease a pizza pan or baking sheet.
- Place the pre-made pizza crust on the greased pizza pan.
- Evenly distribute half the shredded cheddar cheese on the crust.

- Next, scatter the cooked and crumbled bacon over the cheese layer.
- Crack the eggs onto the pizza, ensuring they are evenly distributed across the surface and yolks are not broken.
- Distribute the remaining shredded cheddar cheese evenly over the eggs.
- In the preheated oven, bake the pizza for 12–15 minutes until the crust is golden brown and the cheese is bubbly.
- Remove the breakfast pizza from the oven and let it cool slightly after baking.
- Finally, slice it into wedges and serve hot. Enjoy your homemade breakfast pizza!

## Variations:

- **Veggie Delight**: Add diced bell peppers, onions, tomatoes, or spinach to the pizza for extra flavor and nutrients.
- **Spicy Twist**: Sprinkle red pepper flakes or drizzle hot sauce over the pizza before baking for a spicy kick.
- **Breakfast Veggie Supreme:** Load the pizza with various sautéed vegetables, such as mushrooms, onions, bell peppers, and spinach, for a hearty and nutritious

meal.

- **California Dreaming:** Top the pizza with slices of ripe avocado and diced tomatoes after baking for a fresh and creamy addition.

- **Tex-Mex Fiesta:** Sprinkle cooked and crumbled chorizo or seasoned ground beef over the cheese and eggs, and add sliced jalapeños or diced green chilies for a spicy kick.

(Note: Nutritional values may vary depending on specific ingredients and portion sizes.)

# Creamy Polenta Breakfast Delight

- **Prep Time:** 5 minutes
- **Cook Time:** 20 minutes
- **Total Time:** 25 minutes
- **Servings:** 2
- **Calories**: Approximately 250

## Ingredients:

- 1/2 cup polenta (cornmeal)
- 2 cups water or vegetable broth
- Salt and pepper, to taste
- 1 tablespoon of butter or olive oil
- 1/4 cup grated Parmesan cheese
- Optional toppings: fried or poached eggs, cooked bacon or sausage, sautéed vegetables (such as spinach, mushrooms, or cherry tomatoes), chopped herbs (such as parsley or chives).

## Instructions:

- Over medium-high heat, boil water or vegetable broth in a medium saucepan.
- To prevent lumps, add the polenta gradually while stirring continuously.
- After the polenta thickens and becomes creamy, simmer it on low for 15 to 20 minutes while stirring constantly.
- Add butter or olive oil and grated Parmesan cheese and

mix well. To taste, adjust the amount of salt and pepper.
- Spoon the polenta into two bowls and garnish with the desired ingredients.
- Serve hot, and enjoy your savory breakfast polenta!

## Variations:

- **Mushroom and Thyme:** Sauté sliced mushrooms with garlic and fresh thyme until golden brown. Serve on top of the polenta with a sprinkle of Parmesan cheese.
- **Sun-Dried Tomato and Basil:** Stir chopped sun-dried tomatoes and fresh basil into the cooked polenta. Add a little olive oil and pine nuts on top of it.
- **Cheesy Broccoli:** Steam broccoli florets until tender, then mix them into the polenta with grated cheddar cheese. Sprinkle some red pepper flakes on top as a garnish.
- **Mexican Style:** Put chopped green chilies, diced tomatoes, and black beans into the polenta. Add slices of avocado, salsa, and a dollop of sour cream on top.
- **Italian Sausage and Peppers:** Cook Italian sausage slices and bell pepper strips until browned and tender. Serve over the polenta with a sprinkle of mozzarella

cheese.

(Note: Nutritional values may vary depending on specific ingredients and portion sizes.)

# Minty Melon Smoothie

- **Prep Time:** 5 minutes
- **Cook Time:** 0 minutes
- **Total Time:** 5 minutes
- **Servings:** 2
- Calories: Approximately 100

## Ingredients:
- 2 cups diced honeydew melon
- 1/2 cup plain Greek yogurt
- 1/4 cup of fresh mint leaves
- 1 tablespoon honey or maple syrup (optional)
- 1 cup of ice cubes

## Instructions:
- Place the diced honeydew melon, Greek yogurt, fresh mint leaves, honey or maple syrup (if using), and ice cubes in a blender.
- On high speed, blend for one to two minutes until creamy.
- Check sweetness and add honey or maple syrup if needed.
- If desired, garnish the smoothie in glasses with mint leaves.
- Enjoy your refreshing smoothie immediately!

## Variations:

- **Tropical Twist:** Add 1/2 cup of frozen pineapple or mango chunks for a low-flavor boost.
- **Coconut Cream:** Substitute coconut yogurt for the Greek yogurt and add 2 tablespoons of coconut milk for a creamy coconut flavor.
- **Protein Punch:** Add a scoop of protein powder for an extra protein boost.
- **Citrus Zing:** Squeeze in the juice of half a lime or lemon for a refreshing citrus kick.

(Note: Nutritional values may vary depending on specific ingredients and portion sizes.)

# Kale Chickpea Morning Mix

- **Prep Time:** 5 minutes
- **Cook Time:** 10 minutes
- **Total Time:** 15 minutes
- **Servings:** 2
- **Calories**: Approximately 350

## Ingredients:

- 4 cups kale, washed, stemmed, and chopped
- 1 can (15 ounces) chickpeas, drained and rinsed
- 2 large eggs
- 2 tablespoons of olive oil
- Salt and pepper to taste
- Optional toppings: sliced avocado, cherry tomatoes, feta cheese

## Instructions:

- Add one tablespoon of olive oil to a large skillet over medium heat. Once the skillet has heated up, add the chickpeas and sauté them. Keep stirring them occasionally, making sure they cook evenly. In 5-7 minutes, they should be golden brown and crispy.
- Once cooked, remove the chickpeas from the skillet and set them aside.
- Let the skillet heat up with the remaining tablespoon of olive oil. Add chopped kale to the skillet, sauté it, and

stir it occasionally until it softens and wilts, for about 3 to 5 minutes.

- Put the kale on one side of the skillet and break the eggs on the other. Ensure the eggs are not too close to each other, giving them enough space to cook evenly.
- Continue cooking for 3–4 minutes or until the whites are set but the yolks are still runny. Once cooked, season the eggs and kale to taste with salt and pepper.
- In two separate bowls, separate the chickpeas and sautéed kale. And place a cooked egg in every bowl.
- Add optional toppings like sliced avocado, cherry tomatoes, or feta cheese.
- Serve immediately and enjoy your nutritious breakfast bowl!

## Variations:

- **Spicy Twist:** Add a sprinkle of red pepper flakes or a drizzle of hot sauce for a spicy kick.
- **Grain Addition:** For extra fiber and heartiness, serve the breakfast bowl over cooked quinoa or brown rice.
- **Herb Infusion:** Toss the kale and chickpeas with chopped fresh herbs like parsley or cilantro before

serving for extra flavor.

- **Cheese Lovers:** Sprinkle shredded Parmesan or crumbled goat cheese over the top of the bowl for a cheesy finish.
- **Protein Boost:** Add cooked chicken, turkey sausage, or tofu cubes to the bowl for additional protein.

(Note: Nutritional values may vary depending on specific ingredients and portion sizes.)

## More Then 5 Ingredient Cooking for Two

# Sausage Pancake Breakfast Bake

- **Prep Time:** 15 minutes
- **Cook Time:** 25 minutes
- **Total Time:** 40 minutes
- **Servings:** 2
- **Calories:** Approximately 450

## Ingredients:

- 2 large eggs
- 1/2 cup 2% milk
- 1/4 teaspoon salt
- 1/2 cup all-purpose flour
- 6 ounces of uncooked maple breakfast sausage links
- 1 1/2 tablespoons olive oil
- Optional: butter and maple syrup.

## Instructions:

- Preheat the oven to 425°F (220°C).
- Whisk eggs, milk, flour, and salt in a mixing bowl until smooth and lump-free, 3–4 minutes. Once the batter is ready, set it aside.
- Place a skillet on medium heat to cook sausage links. Cook the sausage links on each side for 5–7 minutes until brown and cooked. After cooking, slice the

sausages into bite-sized pieces. Set them aside.
- Use half a tablespoon of olive oil to grease a small baking dish, like an 8 by 8-inch dish.
- Next, arrange the sliced sausage pieces evenly on the bottom of the greased baking dish.
- Evenly distribute the batter over the sausage pieces. This will ensure the pancake is cooked evenly and has a consistent texture. Use a spatula to eat sausage pieces evenly.
- Place the baking dish in the oven and bake for 20–25 minutes or until the pancake is puffed and golden brown around the edges. Take the pancake out of the oven and let it cool. This will make it easier to slice.
- Finally, slice the pancake into squares and serve it warm. Optionally, you can serve it with butter and maple syrup on the side. Enjoy your delicious and filling breakfast!

## Variations:

- **Cheese Add-In:** Sprinkle shredded cheese over the sausage pieces before pouring the batter for a cheesy twist.

- **Herb Infusion:** Add chopped herbs like parsley or chives to the batter for flavor.
- **Fruit Topping:** Serve with fresh berries or sliced fruit on top for a fruity addition.
- **Nutcracker:** To add a crunchy texture to the batter, mix in chopped nuts, such as pecans or almonds, before baking.

(Note: Nutritional values are approximate and may vary depending on specific ingredients and portion sizes.)

# Ricotta-Berry Crepes

- **Prep Time:** 10 minutes
- **Cook Time:** 15 minutes
- **Total Time:** 25 minutes
- **Servings:** 2
- **Calories:** Approximately 350

## Ingredients:

- 2 large eggs
- 1/2 cup all-purpose flour
- 1/2 cup milk
- 1 tablespoon butter, melted
- 1/2 cup ricotta cheese
- 1 cup mixed berries (such as strawberries, blueberries, or raspberries)
- Powdered sugar, for dusting (optional)
- Maple syrup or honey, for drizzling (optional)

## Instructions:

- First, blend the eggs, milk, and flour until a smooth batter is achieved. Then, stir in the melted butter to the mixture.
- Next, add 1/4 cup of the crepe batter to the nonstick skillet and heat it over medium heat. Swirl the batter in the pan to cover the pan.
- Cook until the edges lift and the bottom is lightly golden, 1-2 minutes.

- Flip and cook the crepe for 1-2 minutes.
- Repeat with the remaining batter to create additional crepes.
- Once you have your crepes, it's time to add the filling. Spread each crepe with a layer of ricotta cheese. Next, add crepe's center with a small handful of mixed berries.
- Fold the crepes in half or roll them up according to your preference. Transfer the crepes to serving plates and dust them with powdered sugar if desired.
- Finally, drizzle them with maple syrup or honey to add a touch of sweetness.
- Serve your delicious ricotta-berry crepes immediately, and enjoy!

## Variations:

- **Nutty Crunch:** Sprinkle chopped nuts (such as almonds or pecans) over the ricotta before adding the berries for texture.
- **Citrus Zest:** Sprinkle lemon or orange zest over ricotta for a citrus kick.
- **Chocolate Indulgence:** Sprinkle chocolate chips or

drizzle melted chocolate over the ricotta and berries for a decadent treat.

- **Coconut Bliss:** Sprinkle shredded coconut over the ricotta and berries for a tropical twist.
- **Cinnamon Spice:** Dust the crepes with ground cinnamon before adding the ricotta and berries for a warm and aromatic flavor.

(Note: Nutritional values are approximate and may vary depending on specific ingredients and portion sizes.)

### **Did you enjoy this book?**

Thank you for purchasing and reading this book. I hope you get a lot out of it.

Can I ask a quick favor, though?

If you enjoyed this book, please leave me a positive review on Amazon.

I love getting feedback from my customers, and reviews on Amazon do make a difference. I read all my reviews and would appreciate your thoughts.

Thanks so much.

**APRIL KELSEY**

**P.S. You can click here to go directly to the book on Amazon and leave your review.**

# **DISCLAIMER**

This 5-Ingredient cooking for two is written to serve as pure information and an educational resource. It is not intended to be medical advice or a medical guide.

Although proper care has been taken to ensure the validity and reliability of the information provided in this book, readers are advised to exercise caution before using any information, suggestions, or methods described.

The writer does not advocate using any of the suggestions, diets, or health programs mentioned in this book. This book is not intended to take the place of a medical professional, a doctor, or a physician. The information in this book should only be used with explicit advice from medically trained professionals, especially in cases where urgent diagnosis and medical treatment are needed.

The author or publisher cannot be held responsible for any personal or commercial damage resulting from misinterpreting or misunderstanding any part of the book.

Made in the USA
Columbia, SC
05 December 2024

48523326R00096